S. Hrg. 113–476

A TRANSFORMATION: AFGHANISTAN BEYOND 2014

HEARING

BEFORE THE

SUBCOMMITTEE ON NEAR EASTERN AND SOUTH AND CENTRAL ASIAN AFFAIRS

OF THE

COMMITTEE ON FOREIGN RELATIONS UNITED STATES SENATE

ONE HUNDRED THIRTEENTH CONGRESS

SECOND SESSION

APRIL 30, 2014

Printed for the use of the Committee on Foreign Relations

Available via the World Wide Web: http://www.gpo.gov/fdsys/

U.S. GOVERNMENT PRINTING OFFICE

91–298 PDF   WASHINGTON : 2015

For sale by the Superintendent of Documents, U.S. Government Printing Office
Internet: bookstore.gpo.gov   Phone: toll free (866) 512–1800; DC area (202) 512–1800
Fax: (202) 512–2104   Mail: Stop IDCC, Washington, DC 20402–0001

CONTENTS

A TRANSFORMATION: AFGHANISTAN BEYOND 2014

WEDNESDAY, APRIL 30, 2014

U.S. SENATE,
SUBCOMMITTEE ON NEAR EASTERN AND
SOUTH AND CENTRAL ASIAN AFFAIRS,
COMMITTEE ON FOREIGN RELATIONS,
Washington, DC.

The subcommittee met, pursuant to notice, at 10:30 a.m., in room SD–419, Dirksen Senate Office Building, Hon. Tim Kaine (chairman of the subcommittee) presiding.

Present: Senators Kaine, Cardin, Risch, Johnson, and McCain.

OPENING STATEMENT OF HON. TIM KAINE, U.S. SENATOR FROM VIRGINIA

Senator KAINE. I want to call the meeting of the Subcommittee on Near Eastern and South and Central Asian Affairs of the U.S. Senate Committee on Foreign Relations to order.

This is an important hearing that we are having today. There will be other members coming and going, as is the norm here in the Senate, and we are very excited to have witnesses here today with us.

I am starting promptly because we have a vote at noon.

We have two very distinguished panels. I want to make sure that we hear from all the witnesses and have an opportunity to engage in dialogue. And so I welcome you all and all members of the public who are here for this important hearing on Afghanistan beyond 2014.

At the turn of the century 2000, few in Afghanistan could have imagined a country where millions of girls were attending school, where Afghan youth enjoyed cell phone access and 75 TV channels at their disposal, where there is a multiethnic Parliament with 70 female Members, actually a higher percentage of women representation than in the United States Congress. Few would have imagined that Afghanistan, whose life expectancy would have grown by more than one-third in a decade, nor could have anyone imagined national elections after three decades of war.

But we have this hearing today recently following April 5, 2014, the beginning of a momentous transition for the people of Afghanistan, the first democratic transfer of power in the history, in the proud history, of that country. We were witnessing a campaign of hope and resilience during that Presidential campaign with high voter turnout, nearly 70 percent. We saw long lines of Afghan voters who wanted to send a powerful message to the Taliban who tried but failed to intimidate them through violence and fear. The vote was the evidence of a strong democratic demand among the Afghan population and the grit and determination of the people.

The election trends are positive. There will be a runoff election. We do not have a favorite in the election, but we rejoice in the turnout and that democratic demand evidenced by high turnout.

There were reports of fraud, although less than in past elections. There was violence, certainly efforts to intimidate, though better than in earlier instances. The challenges are significant both in the completion of this campaign and certainly beyond.

But the elections are an Afghan moment. They also should serve to remind us and the American public of how far Afghanistan has come in the last 13 years.

We hold this hearing today to talk about that. We are not going to gloss over challenges. We will talk about challenges, but we believe this political transition provides a significant opportunity to shift and talk now about the future of the country.

Americans have to know what has been achieved and how an enduring partnership with the Afghan people can ensure that the next decade is as transformative as the last. That is the reason that I wanted to hold this hearing today.

The American people should also always, always take time to be proud of the servicemembers who served in Afghanistan and continue to serve and to our diplomats also and to all from our country who were all ''small A'' ambassadors sacrificing so much to help the Afghan people build a better future.

We saw a horrendous attack last week in Afghanistan that killed three American physicians, and that is a grim reminder of the challenges that remain and the sacrifices that have occurred thus far.

I visited Afghanistan twice, once as Governor to visit my Virginia Guard proudly serving in Afghanistan and once last year with five other Senators to explore the situation as we approached 2014. I have been privileged to meet our troops in the field, in Kabul, and elsewhere and to meet our wonderful State Department, USAID, and other Americans who have helped bring about some significant progress since 2001.

We often debate here in the Senate—and we should—about troop levels in the bilateral security agreement that is no doubt important. We have to support, train, and advise a mission beyond 2014, as do many Afghan political leaders. But today our focus is on other aspects of Afghanistan's transformation. The U.S. Government, the private sector economic development, the NGOs working together in the future to improve the lives of Afghans.

Just a couple of examples. The State Department is working to support the Turkmenistan-Afghanistan-Pakistan pipeline project, and we want to get details about what can be done to facilitate the success of that endeavor.

USAID's Better Than Cash program is working to build an electronic banking system for Afghan citizens.

Farmers have and they need still to have even speedier access to markets for licit agricultural products.

School enrollment for girls is at an unprecedented level. We do not want that to go backward. We want it to go forward.

Life expectancy has increased by two decades. That is a statistic that continually makes me kind of step back and gasp because this is not actuarial math. This is seat-of-the-pants math. But if you basically take a country of 30 million people and you increase life expectancy by 20 years, by my calculation that is 600 million years of additional human life. That is pretty significant. It took the United States about 50 years to make that same move from 1900 until just after World War II. That was an achievement of the last decade in Afghanistan.

Here are some issues that I hope our witnesses will discuss today, and from reading their testimony, I am confident they will. The challenge of youth. The median age in Afghanistan is 18 and the resilience of the democracy rests pretty significantly on the government's ability to engage and then meet in a patient, realistic way the aspirations of Afghan young people.

The Afghan economy and issues along the New Silk Road. I want to thank the Department for making this a priority. Greater economic integration is essential to Afghanistan's future and the neighbors'. And the New Silk Road can be a positive vision for the region's future rooted in the free exchange of goods, people, and ideas.

We are going to have powerful testimony about this today of the empowerment of women. We have to work to ensure that the success and the journey of Afghan women thus far is irreversible and continues.

And lessons learned. What are lessons learned from the experience that we have had in the first 11 or 12 years about things that we have not done well or that others have not done well, NGOs or others, and how can we apply those lessons to improve as we go forward.

The country is on a transformative journey and the people know what is at stake. In January, Colonel Jamila Bayaz, a 50-year-old mother of five, became the first woman to be appointed police chief in Afghanistan. At her promotion ceremony, she said she would not have achieved her position had it not been for the efforts of the United States and the international community.

I do understand—and I think my colleagues hear this as well—a sentiment of exhaustion at home over the long, long, 13 years of war, the longest wars in the history of the United States. And that leads to some exhaustion, and it can lead to a temptation to focus on other issues rather than to continue to be supportive. But we have invested too much of ourselves as a nation to walk away from Afghanistan.

And today we have great witnesses who can share with us things that we can appropriately do, given all the budgetary and other limits we face, things that we can appropriately do that will continue to advance the quality of life in Afghanistan and a strong partnership between our country and the Afghan people.

I was going to ask Senator Risch to do opening comments. I think what I will do is let Senator Risch deliver comments when he appears as the ranking member on this subcommittee. What I will do now with the approval of my colleagues is introduce the first panel and ask you to make opening statements, and then we will move into questions and answers. Again, we are going to try to have both panels up and have a good dialogue by noon so that we can vote at that time.

On the first panel, we have the following.

Jarrett Blanc is Deputy Special Representative for Afghanistan and Pakistan. He has served in this role and as the Special Advisor to the Special Representative since 2009. He has been significantly engaged during this transformative period and we look forward to hearing Mr. Blanc's testimony.

Fatema Sumar is the Deputy Assistant Secretary for South and Central Asia. She joined the State Department in August 2013. Prior to that, she was working on this committee staffing this corner of the world. So she sat in the chairs behind us and this is her first effort to sit and be grilled by committee members. So I encourage my committee members to be tough since this is her first effort in the witness chair. [Laughter.]

But we are very, very glad to have her back to talk about this from the State Department's perspective.

And finally, Kathleen Campbell is the Acting Deputy Assistant to the Administrator for USAID's Office of Afghanistan and Pakistan Affairs. She came from Save the Children where she was associate director of Development Aid Policy and Advocacy.

We are glad to have you, and if you would deliver opening statements in the order I introduced you and then we will move quickly into a good dialogue. Thanks for being here today.

STATEMENT OF JARRETT BLANC, DEPUTY SPECIAL REPRESENTATIVE FOR AFGHANISTAN AND PAKISTAN, U.S. DEPARTMENT OF STATE, WASHINGTON, DC

Mr. BLANC. Thank you very much, Mr. Chairman, members of the committee, and thank you for the opportunity to appear before you today to discuss the future of Afghanistan beyond 2014.

In particular, I would like to thank the members of this committee for your continued support for this mission. The American people have been generous, steadfast, and brave in supporting Afghanistan.

And I would join the chairman in calling attention to the memories of the three American citizens killed last week at the Cure International Hospital in Kabul, not only them, but to the dedication of thousands of American women and men who have served in our Armed Forces and our diplomatic outposts and our assistance programs in Afghanistan.

The investments we have made in Afghanistan have paid important and underreported dividends. We began this mission in late 2001 to prevent Afghanistan from again being used to launch attacks against us. As part of an international coalition of more than 50 nations, we have helped make the world more secure.

Our mission now is to make these gains sustainable by handing over and supporting increasingly capable Afghan institutions. As we approach the end of the ISAF mission and the beginnings of the political transition to a new Afghan Government, I would like to describe evidence that Afghan institutions are precisely that, increasingly capable and sustainable, and to outline the challenges that these institutions now face and the ways in which we and our partners can and intend to continue to help them overcome those challenges.

Afghan confidence and ours begins with the performance of the Afghan National Security Forces, the most highly regarded institution in the country. The Afghan National Security Force has progressed from supporting ISAF operations to conducting them jointly to leading complex operations with ISAF support, and finally in June of last year, to taking the lead for security throughout the country. Since June of last year, they have held their own against the insurgents and have successfully planned and carried out a highly complex effort to protect polls and voters on election day, thwarting Taliban efforts to disrupt the first round of the elections.

The electoral process to date is further reason for measured confidence in Afghanistan's future. For the first time in their history, on April 5 Afghans led every component of the electoral process. The security forces provided the security. The electoral bodies planned and administered the process, meeting nearly every deadline throughout the calendar, and Afghan media provided platforms for reasoned debate about policy and generally avoided inflammatory rhetoric. Afghan political elites formed multiethnic tickets and campaigned all across the country. And most importantly, enthusiasm for the democratic process and hope for their future brought millions of Afghans to the polls despite bad weather and, of course, Taliban threats.

Similarly, Afghan electoral bodies have responded appropriately to allegations of fraud.

Afghan youth, civil society groups, and women all played critical roles in the elections.

The involvement of Afghan women in the elections, in particular, is a sign of a shift in attitude toward women nationwide. And as Secretary Kerry said in his speech at Georgetown last year, if I had to walk blind into a district in Afghanistan and could ask only one question to determine how secure it was and how much progress it was making, I would ask what proportion of girls here are able to go to school. There is no question investing in Afghan women is the surest way to guarantee that Afghanistan will sustain the gains of the last decade and never again be a safe haven for international terrorists.

Sustaining progress through 2014 depends on continued growth of Afghanistan's governance and security institutions and continued support by the international community for a sovereign, stable, unified and democratic Afghanistan. Our assistance programs through the period of transition will remain focused on building the capacity of Afghan institutions to sustain the gains of the last decade, including continued support for Afghan women.

Let me single out three factors in particular that can contribute to sustaining progress in Afghanistan. The first, of course, already mentioned is the bilateral security agreement which could allow for a limited post-2014 mission focused on training, advising, and assisting Afghan security forces and going after the remnants of core al-Qaeda.

Second, the Government of Afghanistan needs to enact policies that will empower the private sector to grow the Afghan economy to make up for decreases in international assistance and to provide jobs for the large population of youth, increase government revenues to overcome the current fiscal gap between revenues and expenditures.

Regional integration, the third factor, will also improve Afghanistan's economic process. And in particular, I would call attention to the Istanbul Process, an Afghan-launched and led mechanism from November 2011 which represents a step forward in terms of dialogue and cooperation between Afghanistan and its neighbors.

The United States has been in Afghanistan for 13 years. We have invested billions of dollars and nearly 2,200 of our service men and women have sacrificed their lives so that extremists who attacked us on September 11 will not again threaten American territory, our citizens, or our allies from Afghan soil. Under President Obama, United States strategy and that of our international partners has aimed at strengthening Afghan institutions so that the Afghan Government and people can provide for their own security, grow their own economy, and manage their own internal and external affairs. The common element in all three of these transitions, security, economic, and political, has been the gradual and responsible transfer of leadership to Afghan hands. That remains our approach and it is working.

Thank you.

[The prepared statement of Mr. Blanc follows:]

PREPARED STATEMENT OF JARRETT BLANC

Chairman Kaine, Ranking Member Risch, members of the committee, thank you for the opportunity to appear before you today to discuss the future of Afghanistan beyond 2014 along with my colleagues, Deputy Assistant Secretary of State for South and Central Asia Fatema Sumar and USAID Deputy Assistant Administrator Kathleen Campbell.

Allow me to begin by thanking the members of the subcommittee for your continued support for our mission. The American people have been generous, steadfast, and brave in supporting Afghanistan. We continue to make great sacrifices, and I would particularly like to honor the memories of the three American citizens killed last week at Cure International Hospital in Kabul along with the dedication of thousands of American men and women who have served in our Armed Forces, our diplomatic outposts, and our assistance programs in Afghanistan.

The investments we have made in Afghanistan have paid important and underreported dividends. We began this mission in late 2001 to prevent Afghanistan from again being used to launch attacks against us. As part of an international coalition of more than 50 nations, we have helped make the world more secure since 2001, and as the major funders of an international civilian assistance effort, we have enabled the Afghans to rebuild their own capacity to provide security, educations, and jobs to their own people and become a reliable partner in efforts to prevent extremists from using their land to launch violence against our people and our allies.

Our mission now is to make these gains sustainable by handing over to and supporting increasingly capable Afghan institutions. As we approach the end of the ISAF mission and the beginnings of the political transition to a new Afghan Government, I would like to describe evidence that Afghan institutions are precisely that—increasingly capable and sustainable—and to outline the challenges that those institutions now face and the ways in which we and our partners can help them to overcome those challenges.

Afghan confidence—and ours—begins with the performance of the Afghan National Security Forces (ANSF), the most highly regarded institution in Afghanistan. As the international community and the Afghan Government together envisioned at the 2010 NATO conference in Lisbon, the ANSF has progressed from supporting ISAF operations to conducting them jointly to leading complex operations with ISAF support to taking over the lead for security throughout the country, which formally took place nearly a year ago in June 2013. Since then they have held their own against the insurgents, secured major events like last fall's Loya Jirga, and successfully planned and carried out a highly complex effort to protect polls and voters on Election Day, thwarting Taliban attempts to disrupt the first round of the elections.

The electoral process to date is further reason for measured confidence in Afghanistan's future. For the first time in their history on April 5, Afghans led every component of the electoral process. Afghan forces provided the security. Afghan electoral bodies planned and administered it, meeting nearly every deadline from candidate registration through release of the preliminary vote tallies. Afghan media provided platforms for reasoned debates about policy and generally avoided inflammatory rhetoric. Afghan civil society organizations and candidate agents monitored the polling centers. Afghan political elites formed multiethnic tickets and campaigned all across the country. Afghan institutions were not flawless but they were responsive, demonstrating significantly increased capacity from the 2004 and 2009 elections. For example, on Election Day, as some polling centers reported running low on ballots, the Independent Election Commission (IEC) tapped prepositioned supplies of contingency ballots and kept the public informed with regular press conferences throughout the day. Most importantly, enthusiasm for the democratic process and hope for their future brought millions of Afghans out to vote despite bad weather and Taliban threats.

Similarly, Afghan electoral bodies have responded appropriately to allegations of fraud. In accordance with electoral laws passed last year, the IEC has quarantined the ballots from centers where it believes further investigation is warranted, the Independent Electoral Complaints Commission (ECC) is adjudicating complaints of fraud, and candidates continue to refer allegations of irregularities to the appropriate authorities. If, as now seems highly likely, a second round is necessary, the competence, transparency, and impartiality of these bodies will be critical in ensuring that the Afghan people broadly accept President Karzai's successor as legitimate and credible.

Afghan youth, civil society groups and women all played critical roles in the elections. Youth were active in all the major Presidential campaigns, reportedly turned out in large numbers to vote, and ran as candidates for many provincial council seats against older incumbents. Afghan civil society groups took responsibility for monitoring the elections, sending 12,000 trained observers to polling centers throughout the country, making sure procedures were followed and filing complaints and alerting news media when they were not. Afghan women also ran for provincial council seats (nationwide, 11 percent of the candidates were women), served as female searchers at polling stations, and also voted in large numbers, especially in urban areas. Nearly 2.5 million Afghan women cast votes, 36 percent of the total. The Afghan Women's Network issued a statement thanking the national security forces for ''providing full support to all women during the election and facilitating a secure environment for people to go vote.''

The involvement of Afghan women in the elections is visible sign of a shift in attitudes toward women nationwide. A recent Democracy International poll found that 92 percent of Afghans believe that women have the right to participate in elections; similarly, the Asia Foundation found that 83 percent of their respondents in Afghanistan said that women should have the same educational opportunities as men. It would be naive to underestimate the considerable social, economic, and legal challenges that still confront Afghan girls and women. These changes have not yet halted violence against women or opened enough schools to girls in every province and it will take many years for them to do so. Still, the elections and the shift in perceptions provide a basis for hope. As Secretary Kerry said in his speech at Georgetown last year: ''If I had to walk blind into a district in Afghanistan and I could only ask one question to determine how secure it was and how much progress it was making, I would ask, 'What proportion of the girls here are able to go to school?' '' There's no question in my mind that investing in Afghan women is the surest way to guarantee that Afghanistan will sustain the gains of the last decade and never again become a safe haven for international terrorists.''

Sustaining progress in Afghanistan after 2014 through the Transformation Decade depends on the continued growth of Afghanistan's governance and security institutions and continued support by the international community for a sovereign, stable, unified, and democratic Afghanistan. This partnership must be based on the principles of mutual respect and mutual accountability and should recognize the increasing responsibility of the sovereign Afghan state and a calibrated reduction of financial and other assistance from the international community. Stability requires Afghan progress on security and political goals which must be matched by effective governance, the advancement of rule of law, human rights, and economic reform. Our assistance programs through this period of transition will remain focused on building the capacity of Afghan institutions to sustain the gains of the last decade, including continued support for Afghan women.

Let me single out three factors in particular that can contribute to sustaining progress in Afghanistan in the next decade. The first is the Bilateral Security Agreement (BSA). The BSA could allow a limited, post-2014 mission focused on training, advising, and assisting Afghan forces and going after the remnants of core al-Qaeda. Such a mission would further strengthen the ANSF in its fight against the Taliban and it would allow us to continue to deny terrorists opportunities to plan attacks against the United States, our interests, and our allies. President Obama has left open the possibility of concluding the BSA later this year with Karzai's successor. Both frontrunners have said publicly that they would sign it soon upon taking office.

Second, the Government of Afghanistan needs to enact policies that will empower the private sector to grow the Afghan economy to make up for decreases in international assistance, provide jobs for its large population of youth, and increase government revenues to overcome the current fiscal gap between revenues and expenditures. The economic challenge is illustrated by flat government revenues over the last 2 years, which reflect a number of factors, including a general slowdown in the economy and hesitation from potential investors (partly a response to uncertainty over the elections and the BSA). The Afghans have taken some steps in recent months to improve revenue collection though there is much work to be done. Corruption remains a fundamental challenge in Afghanistan to governance as well as economic growth—something Afghans themselves recognize. Indeed, both frontrunners have advanced anticorruption agendas during the campaign and both have repeatedly spoken of the need to improve Afghanistan's infrastructure, establish the appropriate legal and security environment to attract foreign investment, and expand educational and technical training opportunities for Afghan youth.

Regional integration, the third factor, will also improve Afghanistan's economic prospects. My colleague, Deputy Assistant Secretary Fatema Sumar, will discuss this topic in detail later in this briefing. However, let me provide some political context for it. The region's stability is inseparable from Afghanistan's stability and prosperity. The Istanbul Process, an Afghan-led mechanism launched in November 2011, represents a step forward in terms of dialogue and cooperation between Afghanistan and its neighbors. This emerging consensus is an important development in terms of the political and security trajectory of Afghanistan.

The United States has been in Afghanistan for 13 years, we have invested billions of dollars, and nearly 2,200 of our service men and women have sacrificed their lives so that the extremists who attacked us on September 11 can never again threaten American territory, our citizens, or our allies from Afghan soil. Under President Obama, U.S. strategy and that of our international partners (as established in conferences in Bonn, Chicago, and Tokyo) has aimed at strengthening Afghan institutions so that the Afghan Government and people can provide for their own security, grow their own economy, and manage their own internal and external affairs. The common element in all three of these transitions—security, economic, and political— has been the gradual and responsible transfer of leadership to Afghan hands. That remains our approach and it is working.

Senator KAINE. Thank you, Mr. Blanc.
Ms. Sumar.

STATEMENT OF FATEMA SUMAR, DEPUTY ASSISTANT SECRETARY, BUREAU OF SOUTH AND CENTRAL ASIAN AFFAIRS, U.S. DEPARTMENT OF STATE, WASHINGTON, DC

Ms. SUMAR. Chairman Kaine, Ranking Member Risch, it is a particular honor for me to be here today given my work on the committee from 2009 to 2013. So thank you for holding this timely hearing and inviting me to testify.

I will summarize my remarks but ask that my written testimony be submitted into the official record.

Senator KAINE. Without objection.

Ms. SUMAR. I will focus today on our efforts to promote regional economic connectivity between Central and South Asia through an initiative that we call the New Silk Road. As you know, Afghanistan has made tremendous strides over the past 12 years. As a result of that progress, the region now has an opportunity to establish a new set of economic, security, and political relationships. This, in turn, will also support sustainable security and stability in Afghanistan.

And I want to underscore that none of this would be made possible without the significant investments made possible in Afghanistan, thanks to the support from the U.S. Congress.

There is no doubt that regional connectivity between Central and South Asia is difficult. This will take many years. It is the least economically integrated region in the world and geopolitical tensions abound. Barriers to trade remain high and many economic reforms are needed. Progress ultimately will depend on the countries themselves deciding that it is in their interests to work together to adopt global best practices.

But despite these many challenges, it is telling that Afghanistan and its neighbors are championing certain aspects of this initiative. They are creating new north-south connections to complement vibrant east-west connections across Eurasia, including those pursued by Russia and China. By supporting their ability to make their own economic choices, we underscore longstanding U.S. support for the independence, sovereignty, and territorial integrity of states in this region.

Under the leadership of Secretary Kerry, our New Silk Road initiative focuses on four key areas. The first is creating a regional energy market, bringing surplus energy from Central Asia to energy-dependent South Asia. The second is improving trade and transport routes across the region. The third is streamlining customs and border procedures to reduce the costs of doing business. And the fourth is connecting people and businesses across the region to connect new regional markets.

By no means is the United States doing all of this alone. In fact, we work in direct partnership with countries in the region, international financial institutions, aid agencies, and others. And our programs complement and support regional priorities such as the Istanbul Process.

Let me turn briefly to the first area, energy, where no sector represents a greater win-win across the region. With a population of more than 1.6 billion people, South Asia's demand for energy is growing. At the same time, Central Asia is a repository of vast energy resources, including oil, gas, and hydropower.

To help create a regional energy market, the United States is supporting multiple projects, including CASA–1000, TUTAP, and TAPI. The World Bank's CASA–1000 project is an electricity transmission line that will enable Tajikistan and Kyrgyzstan to supply 1,300 megawatts of surplus summer hydropower to Afghanistan and Pakistan. The Asian Development Bank's TUTAP electricity project will facilitate the export of electricity from Turkmenistan, Uzbekistan, and Tajikistan to Afghanistan and eventually Pakistan.

These projects have the power to be transformational. For the first time, Central Asia's vast energy resources will be supplied to an energy-dependent South Asia. And the fact that some of this is clean energy is even more compelling.

The United States also supports the Turkmenistan-Afghanistan-Pakistan-India natural gas pipeline, which you mentioned Senator

Kaine, known as TAPI. If ultimately brought to fruition, this project would be a game changer for the Indian subcontinent.

On the second area, trade and transport, we are focused on improving the legal and regulatory frameworks and removing impediments to trade and investments. Bringing states into multilateral trade institutions and getting neighbors to work together are critical steps for cooperation.

On the third area, customs and borders, vibrant markets require functioning transit-trade corridors. We are working with regional partners to reduce border wait times, increase cooperation at key checkpoints and crossings, and prevent the transit of illegal and dangerous material. Our goal is to support open but secure borders throughout the region.

Already trade is picking up as a result. In the last 5 years alone, the volume of intraregional trade in Central Asia has increased by 49 percent. The average cost of crossing borders dropped 15 percent in the last 3 years. And thanks to United States technical assistance, trade is now moving across Afghan borders faster, down from 8 days in 2009 to 3½ hours in 2013.

But ultimately, regional connectivity is about our fourth area, connecting people and businesses. We have funded the studies of hundreds of Central Asian and Afghan students across Central Asia in an effort to build the next generation of leaders, including women. Our women's symposiums in Central and South Asia have brought together women entrepreneurs, private sector partners, and government officials to advance opportunities for women. And we are making real progress connecting our businesses through regional trade forums such as the one we held in Islamabad 2 weeks ago and others in Kazakhstan, Kyrgyzstan, and Bangladesh. With our support, for instance, over 250 Kazakhstani, Uzbekistani, and Afghan businesses gathered in Afghanistan in February where they signed over $8 million in letters of intent for commercial sales.

In conclusion, let me reiterate that while we will continue to face challenges on connecting this region, our New Silk Road initiative is a powerful vision for how Central and South Asia can fully participate in a 21st century global economy and benefit from gains from trade, but also honors the considerable investments Americans have made for over a decade in Afghanistan and the broader region by supporting security and stability for a more prosperous region.

Thank you.

[The prepared statement of Ms. Sumar follows:]

PREPARED STATEMENT OF FATEMA Z. SUMAR

Chairman Kaine, Ranking Member Risch, thank you for inviting me to testify today. It is a particular honor for me to appear before this committee, given my previous experience working on the Senate Foreign Relations Committee. And it is a privilege to speak alongside my colleagues, Jarrett Blanc and Kathleen Campbell, from the State Department and USAID.

Mr. Chairman, the hearing you called today is particularly timely given the historic transition currently underway in Afghanistan, which my colleagues will speak to in greater detail. I will focus my testimony on the broader region to discuss how we are working to promote regional economic connectivity between Central and South Asia to promote greater regional stability and prosperity.

Afghanistan has made tremendous strides over the past 12 years. As a result of that progress, the region has the opportunity to establish a new set of economic, security, and political relationships. This in turn will also support sustainable security and stability in Afghanistan. None of this work would be possible except for the foundation that has been laid by our investments in Afghanistan, thanks to the strong support from Congress. These investments have created the potential for a fundamental improvement in peace and security if we can build on them.

As part of our efforts, the U.S. Government is promoting regional economic connectivity through our New Silk Road initiative. We know that peace and stability are much more likely to be sustained when countries in the region are tied together in trade, when their economies and people share important links.

Mr. Chairman, there is no doubt that regional connectivity between Central and South Asia is difficult and will take many years. This is the least economically integrated region in the world, and geopolitical tensions abound. Barriers to trade remain high, and many economic reforms are needed to realize the full potential of regional cooperation. The international community and private sector can support investments in infrastructure and economic reforms, but progress ultimately will depend on countries themselves deciding it is in their interests to work together and adopting global best practices.

Despite the many real challenges, it is telling that Afghanistan and its neighbors are embracing certain aspects of this initiative, creating new North-South transit and trade routes to complement vibrant East-West connections across Eurasia, including those pursued by China and Russia. Countries in the region know they have more to gain economically by working together than by being isolated. By supporting their ability to make their own economic choices and pursue their own interests, we underline longstanding U.S. support for the independence, sovereignty, and territorial integrity of states in the region.

Under the leadership of Secretary Kerry, our New Silk Road initiative focuses on four areas to link Central Asia with South Asia through Afghanistan by:

    (1) Creating a regional energy market bringing surplus energy from Central Asia to energy-dependent South Asia;

    (2) Improving trade and transport routes across the region;

    (3) Streamlining customs and border procedures to reduce the costs of doing business; and

    (4) Connecting businesses and people across new regional markets.

By no means is the United States doing all of this alone. In fact, we work in partnership with countries in the region, international financial institutions such as the World Bank and Asian Development Bank, aid agencies, and others. And our programs support and complement regional priorities set forth by the Istanbul Process, the Regional Economic Cooperation Conference on Afghanistan (RECCA), and the Central Asia Regional Economic Cooperation Program (CAREC).

ENERGY

Perhaps no sector represents a "win-win" for Central and South Asia more than energy. With a population of more than 1.6 billion people, South Asia's economies are growing rapidly, and in turn South Asia's demand for inexpensive, efficient, and reliable energy is growing. At the same time, Central Asia is a repository of vast energy resources—including oil, gas, and hydropower.

To help create a regional energy market, the United States is supporting the World Bank's CASA–1000 electricity transmission project. When completed, CASA–1000 will enable Tajikistan and Kyrgyzstan to supply 1,300 megawatts of surplus summer hydropower to Afghanistan and Pakistan. CASA has the potential to be transformational. For the first time, Central Asia's vast energy resources will be supplied to an energy-starved South Asia. And the fact that it is clean energy is even more compelling.

We have seen major advances on CASA in the past months. The four CASA countries have made progress in their negotiations to finalize a Power Purchasing Agreement. The World Bank, CASA's lead donor, recently approved its $526 million contribution to CASA. And the U.S. Government has agreed to provide $15 million in project financing for CASA, subject to continued appropriations from Congress. Our contribution should encourage other donors to come forward and fill CASA's remaining funding gap.

We are also working closely with the Asian Development Bank to support its TUTAP electricity project which brings exports of electricity from Turkmenistan, Uzbekistan, and Tajikistan to Afghanistan and eventually Pakistan. By 2018, exports from the Central Asian countries to Afghanistan will reach a capacity of 900 to 1,100 megawatts, with year-round supply from Turkmenistan and Uzbekistan balancing summer supplies from Tajikistan.

The United States also supports the Turkmenistan-Afghanistan-Pakistan-India natural gas pipeline—known as TAPI. If ultimately brought to fruition, this project would be a game changer for the Indian subcontinent. We have a long way to go, and much is dependent on the will and flexibility of the Government of Turkmenistan in taking the necessary steps forward to bring TAPI to the next stage.

TRADE AND TRANSPORT

Improving the legal and regulatory framework, removing impediments to trade and investment, combating corruption and breaking down barriers to trade are necessary preconditions for trade and investment connectivity in the region. Bringing states into multilateral trade institutions and getting neighbors to work together to break down institutional and bureaucratic barriers to trade are critical steps for regional economic cooperation. Cooperation on customs and transit is further advanced by new transit-trade agreements between Afghanistan and its neighbors, under discussion or early in the implementation stage.

This is why the U.S. Government is assisting Afghanistan and Kazakhstan in their efforts to accede to the World Trade Organization (WTO) and helping WTO members Tajikistan and Kyrgyzstan fully realize the benefits of accession. We are also working to operationalize the Afghanistan-Pakistan Transit Trade Agreement (APTTA) and to encourage full implementation of the Cross-Border Transport Agreement between Afghanistan, Kyrgyzstan, and Tajikistan. These agreements hold the potential to dramatically accelerate regional trade.

The United States also works on improving the trade and investment climate throughout the region through our Trade and Investment Framework Agreement (TIFA) talks with Central Asian states, Afghanistan, and Pakistan.

Clearly, one of the biggest obstacles to connecting Central Asia to the rapidly growing markets of South Asia is the barriers between India and Pakistan. Trade normalization between these historic rivals would be a game-changer, signaling to the region and the world South Asia is really open for business. We have been encouraged by positive signs from Islamabad and New Delhi that things may be moving in the right direction, and we are hopeful we will see movement following India's election.

CUSTOMS AND BORDERS

Vibrant markets require functioning transit-trade corridors. Regional economic cooperation with Afghanistan requires a commitment by governments in the region to allow trade to flow across open but secure borders and reduce the costs and time of doing business at the borders.

To support these goals, the United States is working with governments and donor partners to streamline customs procedures and increase cross-border information-sharing throughout the region. The United States supports the ongoing efforts of the European Union's Border Management in Central Asia (BOMCA) and Border Management in Afghanistan (BOMNAF) programs, the Central Asia Border Security Initiative (CABSI), the World Customs Organization, the Organization for Security and Cooperation in Europe (OSCE), and the U.N. Office of Drugs and Crime (UNODC) to improve information-sharing and law enforcement cooperation.

Already, trade is picking up as a result. In the last 5 years, the volume of intraregional trade in Central Asia has increased by 49 percent. The costs of doing business are slowly coming down, with the average cost of crossing borders dropping 15 percent in the last 3 years. And thanks to U.S. technical assistance, customs procedures have been streamlined at seven Afghan border crossing points, resulting in expedited trade with average release time down from 8 days in 2009 to 3½ hours in 2013, saving $38 million annually.

BUSINESSES AND PEOPLE

Ultimately, regional economic connectivity is more than infrastructure, border crossings, and the movement of goods and services. At its heart is the importance of connecting people and businesses across historical, cultural, ethnic, and national borders. The sharing of ideas and expansion of economic markets also creates opportunities for youth and women and strengthens regional stability and prosperity.

This is why the United States has funded the studies of hundreds of Central Asian and Afghan undergraduate and graduate students across Central Asia in an effort to build the next generation of leaders. The U.S.-organized Central Asia-Afghanistan Women's Economic Symposium and South Asia Women's Entrepreneurship Symposium have brought together women entrepreneurs, private sector partners, and government officials to address shared obstacles and advance opportunities for women entrepreneurs.

With U.S. support, over 250 Afghan, Kazakhstani, and Uzbekistani business people gathered in Afghanistan, signing over $8 million in letters of intent for commercial sales. Just 2 weeks ago, Central Asian, Afghan, and Pakistani businesses signed 16 Memorandums of Understanding at the Central Asian Business Opportunities Conference in Islamabad. Similar U.S.-sponsored events in Kazakhstan, Afghanistan, Kyrgyzstan, and Bangladesh have successfully brought together hundreds of South and Central Asian businesses and entrepreneurs, including women, generating millions in trade and fostering important relationships across political, religious, and ethnic lines. We will continue to support programs that connect businesses and people across the region, creating new markets for goods and opportunities for trade and innovation.

CONCLUSION

Mr. Chairman, regional economic connectivity between Central and South Asia is not easy. We will continue to face challenges and setbacks, even as we achieve progress. But the New Silk Road initiative provides the region with a powerful vision for how it can fully participate in a 21st century global economy and benefit from the gains from trade. It also honors the considerable investments Americans have made for over a decade in Afghanistan and the broader region by supporting security and stability for a more prosperous region.

Senator KAINE. Thank you, Ms. Sumar.
Ms. Campbell.

STATEMENT OF KATHLEEN CAMPBELL, ACTING DEPUTY ASSISTANT TO THE ADMINISTRATOR, OFFICE OF AFGHANISTAN AND PAKISTAN AFFAIRS, U.S. AGENCY FOR INTERNATIONAL DEVELOPMENT, WASHINGTON, DC

Ms. CAMPBELL. Chairman Kaine, Ranking Member Risch, and members of the subcommittee, thank you for the opportunity to testify today on the role of USAID in Afghanistan beyond 2014. Our work in Afghanistan is emblematic of our agency's overall mission: USAID partners to end extreme poverty and promote resilient, democratic societies while advancing our security and prosperity. USAID's role in Afghanistan is to promote a stable, inclusive, and increasingly prosperous country.

This is a critical moment in Afghanistan's history, and USAID is working with the Afghan people and our international partners to do all we can to ensure this transition goes as smoothly as possible and that Afghanistan emerges as a stable country on a path toward self-sufficiency.

We understand fully that the fiscal reality our Nation faces at home means that resources available for Afghanistan will decline over time. Weaning Afghanistan from extraordinary levels of assistance is necessary for us and essential for them. To achieve this without triggering a crisis, we must remain a strong partner and continue to provide assistance in areas critical to Afghan development and stability.

I first visited Afghanistan in early 2002 and worked there until 2005. So I know from personal experience that the progress Afghans have made is remarkable but still fragile.

USAID's development assistance, which represents approximately 3 percent of the total military and civilian financial cost of the war in Afghanistan, has helped Afghans achieve gains ranging from a tenfold increase in the number of children enrolled in school to a 20-year increase in life expectancy, as well as a fivefold increase in per capita GDP. The Afghan media is robust. Women have campaigned prominently and turned out in record numbers in this recent election. Parliament increasingly exercises its oversight authority. These are extraordinary gains for a country that in 2002 had virtually no access to reliable electricity, roads, or modern communications and disadvantaged almost half of its population, its women and girls, by prohibiting them from contributing to Afghan society and the economy.

USAID's strategy going forward calls for making durable the significant achievements in health, education, and women, focusing on economic growth and fiscal sustainability to mitigate the economic impact of the troop withdrawal, and the declining levels of donor assistance, and supporting legitimate and effective Afghan governance and, in turn, promoting stability. USAID has also adjusted its implementation model to meet the challenges of transition.

While significant progress has been made to date, there is still much to be done to strengthen the critical role that women, youth, and civil society play in Afghanistan's future. USAID is supporting women including through the launch of USAID's largest gender program which will empower women to participate fully in the economic, political, and civil society sectors.

In recognition of the fact that youth are integral to the future stability of Afghanistan, USAID is supporting the provision of market-driven job skills, business training, access to credit, business development support, and job placement services.

USAID's assistance also supports the development of a strong and active civil society to enhance the political process, solve community problems, and advocate for good governance. With USAID's support, civil society organizations have played a critical role in the 2014 election to date.

Direct assistance to the Afghan Government is used to build the Afghan Government's ability to sustain these investments and gains that have been made and to reduce its dependence on donors. All direct assistance to the Afghan Government is subject to strict safeguards and oversight.

To ensure strong oversight of United States assistance funds, USAID developed the Accountable Assistance for Afghanistan, or A3 initiative, which, combined with standard USAID oversight measures, prevents funds from being diverted from their development purpose by malign actors. We do not assume that there is any level of acceptable waste, fraud, or abuse in our programs.

In conclusion, to secure our overall national security objectives, USAID remains committed to ensuring that the remarkable progress made in Afghanistan is sustained and made durable. The risks and the sacrifices that the people of the United States have made in Afghanistan and the determination of the Afghan people, particularly women, demand no less.

I look forward to answering any questions you have. Thank you.

[The prepared statement of Ms. Campbell follows:]

PREPARED STATEMENT OF KATHLEEN CAMPBELL

Chairman Kaine, Ranking Member Risch, and members of the subcommittee, thank you for allowing me the opportunity to testify before you today to discuss the role of the U.S. Agency for International Development (USAID) in support of U.S. civilian development efforts in Afghanistan looking at 2014 and beyond. Our work in Afghanistan is emblematic of our agency's overall mission: USAID partners to end extreme poverty and promote resilient, democratic societies while advancing our security and prosperity. USAID's role in Afghanistan is to promote a stable, inclusive, and increasingly prosperous country. During the past decade, Afghanistan has made remarkable development gains across multiple sectors, thanks to the whole-of-government efforts of the United States, along with our international partners, the Afghan Government and the Afghan people. It is an honor to appear before you today with Deputy Assistant Secretary of State for South and Central Asian Affairs Fatema Sumar, and Deputy Special Representative for Afghanistan and Pakistan Jarrett Blanc.

2014 is a pivotal year for Afghanistan as the country navigates a series of three transitions: the first democratic transfer of power in Afghanistan's history; the completion of the security transition, including the withdrawal of a majority of international troops; and the continuing effort to reduce Afghanistan's reliance on international aid by facilitating private sector-led economic growth. This is a critical moment in Afghanistan's history, and USAID is working with the Afghan people and our international partners to do all we can to ensure these transitions go as smoothly as possible, and that Afghanistan emerges as a stable country on a path toward self-sufficiency.

We understand fully that the fiscal reality our Nation faces at home means that resources available for Afghanistan will decline over time. Weaning Afghanistan from extraordinary levels of assistance is necessary for us, and essential for them. To achieve this without triggering a crisis, we must remain a strong partner and continue to provide assistance in areas critical to Afghan development and stability. To do this with fewer resources, we are making tough decisions and prioritizing investments that have the greatest potential for long-term sustainability. As USAID navigates through the 2014 transition period and beyond, we are committed to expending every effort to safeguard taxpayer funds and ensure that the development progress in Afghanistan is maintained and made durable.

Looking to 2015 and beyond, USAID will continue to pursue America's goal of an inclusive, stable Afghanistan, and to support Afghanistan's goals, as described in the Afghan National Priority Programs, the bilateral Strategic Partnership Agreement and at the Tokyo Conference in July 2012. These goals include increased Afghan ownership of their development, reduced dependence on foreign aid, improved delivery of services by the Afghan Government, and the promotion of democracy, fundamental freedoms, and human rights. Afghanistan has made important progress in key areas like establishing a sound electoral framework and improving budget transparency. While much more progress is needed in various areas, the political transition represented by the Presidential election presents an opportunity for further reforms.

In support of these goals for Afghanistan, USAID's strategy going forward calls for making durable the significant achievements in health, education, and for women; focusing on economic growth and fiscal sustainability to mitigate the economic impact of the troop withdrawal and declining levels of civilian assistance; and supporting legitimate and effective Afghan governance, and in turn promoting stability.

I first visited Afghanistan in early 2002 and lived and worked there until 2005 as head of the International Rescue Committee in Afghanistan. In 2002 when I arrived, buildings were in ruin throughout the city; wrecked planes littered the airport; there were no phones, few shops, and three currencies; driving through the Shomali plain outside Kabul, red stones edged the highway warning people away from fields of land mines scattered amongst destroyed grape vines and orchards. Afghanistan has made considerable progress over the ensuing 12 years. Afghan businesses are now exporting an increasing number of agriculture commodities; Afghans have become active participants in their government, making their voices heard in elections while advocating for needed reforms; and they have experienced tremendous gains in access and quality of health and education services.

I bring these perspectives to USAID's work today, and I know from personal experience that the dramatic progress Afghans have made is remarkable, yet still fragile. That is why USAID has been planning and adjusting its programming for years in anticipation of the transitions in 2014, to maximize sustainability and ensure oversight and accountability of the resources the American people have provided in support of Afghanistan.

USAID IMPACT AND RESULTS

USAID's development assistance, which represents approximately 3 percent of the total military and civilian financial cost of the war in Afghanistan, has helped Afghans achieve gains ranging from a tenfold increase in the number of children enrolled in school, to a 20-year increase in life expectancy, as well as fivefold increase in per capita GDP. These are extraordinary gains for a country that in 2002 had virtually no access to reliable electricity, roads or modern telecommunications, and disadvantaged almost half of its population—women and girls—by prohibiting them from contributing fully to Afghan society and the economy. Specific examples of how USAID has supported meaningful gains in Afghanistan that have contributed to extraordinary results are as follows:

- Health: Life expectancy has increased from 42 years to over 62 years since 2002; the maternal mortality rate has declined by 80 percent from 1,600 to 327 deaths per 100,000 births; and child mortality decreased by 44 percent from 172 to 97 deaths per 1,000 live births.
- Education: In 2002, there were approximately 900,000 Afghan children in school, and virtually none were girls. Today, approximately 8 million children are registered to attend school and more than one-third of them are girls.
- Economic Growth: Afghan Government revenues have more than doubled from 2002 to 2013. Revenue from customs has been the fastest growing segment, increasing over 400 percent since 2006. The estimated Afghan GDP in 2011 was $23.6 billion, more than six times higher than in 2002, representing a 9 percent per year average increase. Afghanistan's overall ranking in the 2014 World Bank/IFC ''Doing Business'' Index improved from 170 to 164 (out of 189 countries).
- Mobile Technology: in 2002, there were few fixed telephone lines and making calls outside of Afghanistan required a satellite phone. Today, the combined phone network covers 90 percent of the Afghan population. Eighty-five percent of women have access to a mobile phone. The telecommunications sector is Afghanistan's greatest source of foreign direct investment, largest remitter of taxes to the government, and biggest licit employer, providing jobs for 100,000 Afghans.

The Afghan people recognize the progress that has been made. For the past 9 years, The Asia Foundation, with support from USAID, has conducted a nationwide survey of Afghan attitudes and opinions, tracking trends among the population. The results of the 2013 survey show the impact these gains are making. Fifty-seven percent of all Afghans said they believe their country is moving in the right direction. This number has increased steadily since 2008, when it stood at 38 percent. Not surprisingly, the vast majority—88 percent—said they were better off economically than they were under the Taliban. Five in six Afghans—men and women—believe that women should have an education. Seventy-five percent believe it is acceptable to criticize the government in public—a sign of an active democracy with an independent media, which is the civilian institution in which Afghans have the most confidence.

Afghanistan has also made significant gains in governance, though much more is needed. Afghanistan enacted a constitution in 2004 that enshrines democratic principles, women's rights, and freedom of expression. The Afghan media is robust, diverse, and independent. Afghanistan's Parliament is 25 percent female and women have campaigned prominently and turned out in record numbers in this recent election. The Parliament increasingly exercises its oversight authority over key appointments and over the budget. More reforms are needed, but the basic foundation of self-governance is strong.

USAID MOVING FORWARD

USAID understands the challenges facing Afghanistan. In anticipation of this transitional year, as well as 2015 and beyond, USAID has regularly reviewed and adjusted its programs to ensure that they advance the strategic objectives of the United States and are achievable and sustainable. USAID's strategy in Afghanistan is threefold:

- Maintaining and making durable the gains made in health, education, and for women;
- Supporting continued economic growth and employment through a focus on the agriculture sector and private sector development, operations and maintenance of infrastructure investments, and responsibly developing the extractives industry, all key to ensuring future fiscal sustainability; and,
- Fostering legitimate and effective Afghan governance, including support for the 2014 Presidential and 2015 parliamentary elections, the rule of law, and a robust civil society.

Operationally, USAID has adjusted its implementation model to improve sustainability and meet the challenges presented by the transition.

- Developing a multitiered monitoring strategy to address reduced mobility and decreased field staff that, along with other monitoring and evaluation efforts, will continue to ensure appropriate oversight of projects;

- Transforming USAID's approach in Afghanistan to one of mutual accountability that incentivizes Afghan reforms by conditioning an increasing percentage of our assistance to the government on progress on reforms and that continues to increase government involvement and ownership of development needs; and
- Focusing on long-term sustainability through implementing USAID policies on sustainability, including the principles of: (1) increasing Afghan ownership and capacity; (2) contributing to community stability and public confidence in the Government of Afghanistan; and (3) implementing effective and cost-efficient programming.

USAID is also focusing its assistance to encourage regional integration to strengthen economic ties between Afghanistan and its neighbors in an effort to bring greater prosperity and also greater stability to the region. USAID is laying the groundwork for a more economically connected region by facilitating trade, providing technical assistance for regional energy projects such as the World Bank's Central Asia and South Asia (CASA)-1000 project, promoting business-to-business networking and helping countries address other border issues, including countering trafficking in persons.

For example, USAID's Afghanistan Trade and Revenue project is working with the Government of Afghanistan to achieve World Trade Organization accession, promote trade agreements and private sector linkages throughout South and Central Asia, and to strengthen the government's ability to generate revenue from trade and legitimate taxation. Just 2 weeks ago, USAID sponsored the Central Asian Business Opportunities Conference in Islamabad, a business-to-business networking event that included over 300 participants from Pakistan, Afghanistan, and the five Central Asian countries. Progress was made on some of the technical challenges of regional trade. We will continue to engage on building regional economic linkages at the Astana Economic Forum next month. This effort requires developing technical know-how, political agreement, and, in some cases, physical infrastructure, agreements, and policies that meet international standards. It is one of the ways we are assisting Afghanistan stand on its feet as a viable economic partner in its region.

USAID is constantly reviewing and evaluating its portfolio to ensure maximum impact in coordination with the U.S. Government interagency and the Afghan Government, including through a semiannual portfolio review process. For example, as a result of internal USAID reviews and in consultation with the Afghan Government, USAID determined that an activity supporting access to credit for agriculture in southern Afghanistan was not delivering the desired results. USAID de-scoped that activity and reprogrammed the funds to other elements of the program that continue to deliver results. The lessons learned from that agriculture activity have helped inform the design of new USAID agriculture programs that focus on strengthening value chains throughout Afghanistan. We are also leveraging the ongoing work and expertise of our colleagues at the Commerce Department, the Overseas Private Investment Corporation, and the Office of the U.S. Trade Representative, to ensure a coordinated and effective effort.

SUPPORTING WOMEN, YOUTH, AND CIVIL SOCIETY IN AFGHANISTAN

While significant progress has been made to date, there is still much work to be done in Afghanistan related to strengthening the critical role that women, youth, and civil society play in Afghanistan's governance and its future.

Women

Women, while much more active in society than in 2001, still face many challenges. The Asia Foundation Survey found that the most pressing problems for women, as identified by Afghans, include education and illiteracy, lack of job opportunities for women, and women's legal rights. Looking to 2015 and beyond, USAID is aiming to solidify gains for women by further integrating them into projects across all of the sectors in which USAID works to ensure their access to increased opportunities for economic independence, education, improved health, and participation in democratic processes. USAID is supporting these opportunities in a number of ways, including through the launch of USAID's largest gender program in the world, known as "Promote." This program will develop a cadre of educated Afghan women between the ages of 18 and 30, empowering them to fully participate in the economic, political, and civil society sectors of Afghan society: it will help women establish and/or expand small- to medium-sized businesses; help civil society organizations increase their knowledge and skills so they can better support women's rights, outreach and advocacy campaigns; facilitate fellowships with relevant Afghan Government ministries and agencies with a goal of achieving a critical mass of women in the civil service; and train women in the public, private, and civil service sectors in management and leadership. In addition to Promote, Afghanistan is in the vanguard of USAID's agencywide Gender Equality and Female Empowerment policy, which requires that all USAID projects undergo gender analyses to identify gender-based disparities in access to opportunities. To date, more than 40 gender analyses have been completed in Afghanistan, to determine how best to integrate women into USAID projects across all sectors. These efforts compliment the work of other agencies such as the U.S. Trade Representative, which signed Memorandum of Understanding on Joint Efforts to Enable the Economic Empowerment of Women and Promote Women's Entrepreneurship with the Government of Afghanistan last year.

Youth

Afghanistan is facing a rapidly growing population and out of a population of almost 30 million people, 68 percent are under the age of 25. In recognition of the fact that youth are integral to the future stability of Afghanistan, USAID is providing support to this segment of society by improving access to education, increasing technical and vocational education and training opportunities, and establishing 2- and 4-year post-secondary programs. In addition to working with the Afghan Government to improve the relevance of academic programs to the labor market, USAID is aiming to increase the provision of market-driven job skills and business training, access to credit, business development support, and job placement services. Through its Afghanistan Workforce Development Program, USAID projects that 25,000 Afghans will be trained and/or placed in jobs, many of whom will be women and youth.

Civil Society

A vibrant civil society in Afghanistan is critically important to establishing effective bridges between the Afghan Government and citizens, serving as active observers and watch dogs, and participating in government policymaking and service delivery through robust advocacy. USAID's assistance supports the development of a strong and active civil society sector to help Afghan citizens more effectively participate in the political process, solve community problems, and advocate for good governance. With USAID support, civil society organizations have played a critical role in the 2014 election to date, deploying thousands of election observers across the country. Civil society organizations have also played an unprecedented role in organizing citizens across the country to identify their top priorities for the next administration and distilling those priorities into a candidate pledge, which was signed by a majority of Afghan Presidential candidates. These candidates committed themselves to support policy recommendations involving peace and stability, social and economic development and human rights and good governance. This is the first time a Presidential candidate pledge has been utilized in Afghanistan at this scale. Looking to 2015 and beyond, USAID will continue to help strengthen the gains civil society has made to date.

OVERSIGHT AND ACCOUNTABILITY

USAID has learned important lessons over its 12-year engagement, and has drawn on experiences in other challenging environments, including Iraq, Pakistan, Yemen, Sudan, and Colombia, to ensure strong oversight of U.S. assistance funds.

In addition to standard USAID oversight measures implemented worldwide, USAID has implemented the Accountable Assistance for Afghanistan (A3) initiative, designed to prevent funds from being diverted from the development purpose to malign actors. Some of the approaches USAID employs under A3 include:

1. Award Mechanisms—We rely less on large agreements and have increased the number of smaller and more flexible agreements. We are also utilizing assistance awards that provide the most visibility on project costs, such as cost-reimbursable contracts and limiting layers of subcontracts to two.

2. Partner Vetting—The USAID Mission established a Vetting Support Unit in February 2011. The unit conducts checks on non-U.S. companies and non-U.S. key individuals for prime contractors, subcontractors, grant recipients and subgrantees to determine whether or not they are associated with known malign entities or individuals. We have kept over $49 million from being awarded to those who did not meet our vetting requirements.

3. Financial Controls—We are enhancing controls on project funds, such as using electronic funds transfers in lieu of cash payments, using independent financial monitors to verify appropriate usage of funds, ensuring close review of recipients' claims prior to payment, and performing audits of locally incurred cost.

4. Project Oversight—USAID uses a multitiered monitoring approach that includes, as appropriate, independent monitoring contractors; observation by U.S.

Government staff; reporting by implementing partners, local nongovernmental organizations and civil society; and use of technological tools, such as time- and date-stamped photos. By using multiple sources of monitoring data, USAID can compare information received from separate sources to ensure the greatest degree of oversight possible.

USAID's multitiered monitoring approach focuses on gathering and analyzing multiple sources of data across those tiers in order to compare information and ensure confidence in reporting data, allowing USAID to use the results to make further programmatic decisions. Supporting this approach is the new Implementation Support Team (IST). This team is charged with providing an additional layer of critical review and analysis, on a cross-sectoral basis, for the streams of monitoring information collected and for providing USAID leadership and program managers with advice for addressing challenges in project implementation.

Building on past monitoring and evaluation activities in Afghanistan, USAID has recently issued a request for proposals for the new Monitoring Support Project. This request was issued following extensive consultations with international donors, Congress, and implementing partners as well as a comprehensive analysis of USAID's experience using independent monitoring around the world. This project will utilize a variety of monitoring methods to verify project data, including site visits, GPS and time/date stamped photos, interviews, and crowd-sourcing. Independent monitoring, however, is not the sole source of monitoring data. And, it will not take the place of USAID staff as project managers. Instead, it is one tool that USAID can use to validate reporting data from other sources. Should USAID determine that its multitiered monitoring approach cannot provide adequate oversight over project activities, it will not hesitate to terminate or de-scope projects.

Audits provide useful oversight and discipline, and complement and reinforce USAID's own efforts to ensure U.S. tax dollars are used effectively and efficiently. There are currently over 100 on-going audits of USAID programs in Afghanistan. In fiscal year 2013, the U.S. Government Accountability Office, USAID Office of Inspector General, and the Special Inspector General for Afghanistan Reconstruction completed over 65 financial and program audits in Afghanistan.

Although there are inherent risks in doing business in a country like Afghanistan, we prioritize the effective and accountable use of taxpayer dollars and do not assume that there is any level of acceptable fraud, waste, or abuse in our programs. This means that oversight must be a process of continual re-examination of ongoing efforts, and that there must be flexibility to adjust to new circumstances as they arise.

DIRECT ASSISTANCE IN AFGHANISTAN

Direct assistance to the Afghan Government is used to build the Afghan Government's ability to sustain the investments and gains that have been made over the last decade and to reduce its dependence on donors. As the U.S. transitions its programs in Afghanistan, Afghanistan must continue to build its capacity to govern and provide services to its people. Providing funds directly is a critical way in which to accomplish this goal. At the same time, USAID has put in place stringent measures to safeguard taxpayer funds, and only works with those Afghan ministries in which USAID believes it can responsibly mitigate risk. This is in keeping with commitments made by both the previous and current U.S. administrations to increase our work through local governments and organizations, not just in Afghanistan but around the world. Such work is critically important to fulfill the ultimate goal of assistance, namely helping countries stand on their own two feet.

USAID implements direct assistance in Afghanistan through two mechanisms: multilateral trust funds, such as the Afghanistan Reconstruction Trust Fund (ARTF) managed by the World Bank, and through bilateral direct assistance agreements with specific Afghan ministries. Of the approximately $17.5 billion in obligated USAID funds for Afghanistan since 2001, about 5 percent, or $770 million, is allocated for direct assistance with the Afghan Government, of which USAID has disbursed $283 million. About half of all funds thus far disbursed are for health sector programming. USAID only disburses money as direct assistance to the Afghan Government after substantial conditions are met to ensure the funds will be responsibly and accountably managed and tracked.

USAID has a rigorous system of oversight for its direct assistance programming with the Afghan Government. USAID conducts assessments to identify the strengths and weaknesses of each ministry for which a direct assistance project is being contemplated. These assessments review a ministry's basic procurement, financial and human resource systems and are followed by a USAID-conducted internal assessment of the risks associated with working with the ministry. To date,

USAID has contracted accounting firms to conduct 16 ministry assessments. From these assessments, USAID has decided to provide direct assistance to seven ministries to implement a specific project. After the assessment and review, we then build our mitigating measures and safeguards accordingly to each project that we conduct with the specific ministry or agency to ensure risks associated with the project are mitigated. At the same time, through technical assistance, we also seek to build Afghan systems that will be able to prevent fraud, waste, or abuse on their own.

For direct assistance, USAID utilizes multiple levels of protection to mitigate risks to taxpayer funds. These measures may include, but are not limited to:

- Requiring the establishment of a noncommingled, separate bank account for each project with USAID;
- Disbursement of funds only after USAID has verified that the ministry has achieved a performance milestone or USAID has verified incurred costs;
- An annual audit by a USAID OIG-approved firm;
- Substantial involvement and oversight by USAID staff in procurement processes;
- Independent management, monitoring, and evaluation of services; and
- Technical assistance through other projects to increase the capacity of ministries while addressing any vulnerabilities or weaknesses identified in the assessments.

All direct assistance requires compliance with USAID accountability and oversight procedures, including site visits. Ministries are required to fully comply with the conditions precedent prior to and throughout the disbursement process. If Afghan ministries fail to adhere to these conditions, the agreements are subject to immediate suspension or termination.

For example, USAID has worked closely with Afghanistan's energy utility, Da Afghanistan Breshna Sherkat (DABS), to assess its financial management systems, audit its progress and monitor results. USAID negotiated a series of preconditions and financial controls pursuant to the launch of a $75 million program to install a turbine at Kajaki dam. In addition to the tight financial controls implemented with DABS, USAID has been involved in every step of the procurement and implementation process to ensure that results are being delivered as planned. Payments of $1.6 million have been made by DABS to the implementing contractors only after being verified financially and technically as appropriate for the delivery of the goods or services in question. This project also includes a phased approach, with increasingly more significant parts of the project being undertaken only after a thorough review of the previous phase to ensure both financial and technical aspects of the project proceed properly.

CONCLUSION

USAID understands the risks and the sacrifices that Americans, our troops, diplomats, and their families take every day to serve in Afghanistan, whether in a military capacity, as a government civilian, or as an implementing partner. Since 2001, 434 people working for USAID partner organizations in Afghanistan have been killed and another 768 wounded.

Throughout our efforts, we are applying important lessons from the past 12 years in Afghanistan, as well as from other high-risk environments in which USAID has worked. As USAID navigates through the 2014 transition period and looks to 2015 and beyond, we are committed to expending every effort to safeguard taxpayer funds and ensure that the remarkable development progress in Afghanistan is maintained and made durable, in order to secure our overall national security objectives. It is an honor to be able to share with you today a small glimpse of what USAID is doing in that regard. I look forward to answering any questions that you may have.

Senator KAINE. Thank you, Ms. Campbell.

With the two great panels and votes beginning at noon, we will do a 6-minute round of questions, one round for the first panel. We will leave the record open for written questions. We will then move to the second panel.

For this panel, let me begin with the issue of women's empowerment and any potential backsliding. As recently as February, there were efforts by certain elements in the Afghan political system to weaken laws on the books protecting the rights of women and girls.

Human Rights Watch has particularly warned about concerns of backsliding in this area.

What do you think of the likely direction of this trend and how can the United States engage with the new government on this issue? You have referred to it briefly, but I am interested in your thoughts on the trend and what specifically we can do to make sure it goes in the right direction. Please, Ms. Campbell.

Ms. CAMPBELL. Thank you.

As you noted, women have made tremendous progress. We believe that the educational services that we have been helping the Afghan Government to provide is one of the best measures that we can take to ensure that the progress women have made is respected and maintained.

As I noted in my testimony, one of the largest programs USAID has ever designed for women is about to be launched this summer. The Promote project will build on the gains we have made in educating girls and will target women with secondary education to become the future leaders of Afghanistan. The support we will be providing will focus on helping this cohort to become leaders in the economy, leaders in government, leaders in civil society, providing support to civil society groups who can advocate on behalf of human rights and women's rights. So we are confident there will be a voice for women, by women, and by supportive men in the future.

Senator KAINE. Mr. Blanc.

Mr. BLANC. Senator, thank you. If I could just add some of our political work, in addition to our programmatic work. I think, first of all, it is important to note in the case that you just described of the potential for legal backsliding earlier this year, that it really was Afghan women who mobilized to prevent that law from being enacted and successfully ran a campaign that got the legislature or got the executive engaged and defeated the effort. And I think that is exactly the kind of thing that we hoped to see and are glad to be seeing in the politics of Afghanistan.

The second thing that I would note is that the international community has been very clear, going back through perhaps the Lisbon Conference and then moving through a variety of fora, the Tokyo Conference, the Chicago NATO summit, the Bonn Conference, that the assistance that Afghanistan needs is very much contingent on continued progress in a number of areas, including continued progress on the rights and role of women. And I think it is something that Afghans broadly understand and I hope contributed to the successful effort earlier this year.

Senator KAINE. While we are on the subject of the international support for the Afghan effort, why do you not give us an update on the current status of the Tokyo Mutual Accountability Framework and how you see that developing once the Presidential elections are through.

Mr. BLANC. The Tokyo Mutual Accountability Framework has both some high-level aspirations and some very specific responsibilities for the Government of Afghanistan. And I think that as we expected in Tokyo, we are seeing better progress in some areas than in others. We are very pleased, for example, to see a more transparent budget process. We are very pleased to see a better process for sharing budgetary decisions with the provinces. And of course, we are especially pleased to see the implementation of all of the agreed steps in the Tokyo Framework in the runup to the election.

There are other areas where there is still work to be done, for example, in passing a new mining law. And I think one thing that we have been very careful about is to remind not just the current administration but all of the candidates and the people who are likely to continue to play significant roles in Afghanistan in the next administration, that this is the set of expectations that we have agreed to—we in the international community and the Afghans—and we are not really expecting a change from that in the early days of a new administration.

Senator KAINE. Other comments on the framework?

[No response.]

Senator KAINE. Let me ask one additional comment about the most recent elections. To what degree was the democratic demand that was seen in the sizeable turnout expressed in terms of a desire to reduce corruption in the country, and what do you see about anticorruption efforts going forward?

Mr. BLANC. I will quickly start and just say that all of the major candidates and certainly the two candidates who now appear to be possibly moving forward to a second round made anticorruption and governance a central part of their campaign, and both have signed broad anticorruption pledges. So I think it is very clear that the Afghan people are demanding an improvement in governance and a reduction in corruption. And that is something where again, as was the case in the women's issue earlier this year, our role is increasingly to support Afghan domestic politics in doing the right thing.

Senator KAINE. Other comments? Kathleen.

Ms. CAMPBELL. Yes. I would just add that the United States is happy to see that it is civil society—it is the Afghan people—who are stepping up and speaking out on these issues. It is one of the things that USAID is providing support for—to build the capacity of civil society in this area. The media, I think, has also had a very important role in ensuring transparency, increasing transparency regarding the Afghan Government's activities.

Some of our work with Afghan Government institutions is also focused on strengthening their systems so that they are less subject to corruption, and increasing the transparency of those institutions.

Senator KAINE. Thank you very much.

Senator Risch.

Senator RISCH. Thank you, Mr. Chairman.

Mr. Blanc, I represent Idaho and I have a constituent that is being held by the Taliban, as you know. His name is Bo Bergdahl. And people in Idaho read with interest and indeed with concern the recent news reports about the fact that the Haqqani network was holding him. The Taliban want to release him, but because of the fragmented situation as far as the United States is concerned between the DOD, Department of State, et cetera, they are having difficulty doing this. This caused a great deal of concern.

Having said that, I know who we are dealing with, and I under-stand that there are answers to these things. So I want to give you this public opportunity to put a fence around this and explain to my constituents in Idaho and to America how hard all of you work to try to get people like this released and particularly Mr. Bergdahl. So I would like, if you could, please to give us some reassurances in that regard.

Mr. BLANC. Senator, thank you very much for the opportunity to respond to that story which, as you indicate, we view as entirely inaccurate.

Our hearts go out to Sergeant Bergdahl's family. Our hearts go out to Sergeant Bergdahl. He has been gone for far too long. And we and our colleagues across the Government in the Department of Defense, in the intelligence communities, elsewhere are striving in the most energetic and creative ways we can devise to try to secure his release. Speaking for my office, I can say without qualification that nothing energizes the efforts of our office so much as Sergeant Bergdahl.

Unfortunately, the Taliban broke off direct contact with us in January 2012. We would very much like to return to direct contact with them, and if we do, at the top of our agenda will be Sergeant Bergdahl.

It is certainly not the case, as was reported, that somehow the Taliban and Haqqani network are seeking to release him and that interagency squabbles within the United States Government are preventing or delaying that.

Senator RISCH. Mr. Blanc, thank you very much. I continue to be impressed with what a high priority this is for the State Department, for DOD, and I appreciate how well you keep in touch with us and in touch with those who need to know these kinds of things. We appreciate your efforts and we are all going to work together to see if we cannot make this happen as soon as possible. Thank you.

Thank you, Mr. Chairman.

Senator KAINE. Thank you, Senator Risch.

I am going to violate a rule and ask another question or two in case one of the colleagues wants to come back, and then we will move to the second panel.

Talk a little bit about the relationship, the economic prospects between Afghanistan and Pakistan. That has been a very challenged relationship. And yet, they are in a regional economy where greater licit economic trade could be to the benefit of both. This pipeline project is an example of something that could be a tangible. If you would talk a little bit about the prospects there, I think that would be helpful.

Ms. SUMAR. Thank you for that question, Senator Kaine.

So as you know, as we think about the region, one of things we are really struck by is the real willingness in leadership that we are seeing from the countries themselves to actually find more creative ways to engage and not to be trapped by their own geography, so to speak. And so we are seeing this in different types of markets, and one is the energy market, as you rightly pointed out. We have seen more movement in the last 6 months, I would say, than we have had in 6 years or so on electricity transmissions in particular. And so projects such as CASA–1000, which is this electricity transmission line that would go from Kyrgyzstan and

Tajikistan to Afghanistan and then to Pakistan has really galvanized I think cooperation and negotiations among these countries in a way that they really have not had these discussions and negotiations before.

I think CASA–1000 would make a great Harvard School of Business study actually, not just for this particular project of electricity lines, but looking at how these countries are willing to work together for a common future.

What really strikes me here is there is a common need here which is in this case energy generation and the need for more energy for Pakistan, for India, for the broader South Asia Continent. Water is literally spilling in Tajikistan, for instance. However, the Tajiks are not making any money off of the excess water they have, particularly in the summer months. So if there is a way to create the hydro potential, both to upgrade existing facilities but also to create new transmission lines that can bring excess, surplus hydro down from the Central Asian states into Afghanistan where Afghanistan benefits both as a recipient where it will keep 300 megawatts off the grid and also to capture revenue fees from the transit of 1,000 megawatts into Pakistan, it creates multiple opportunities for these countries.

And so we have had really positive momentum. The World Bank brought CASA–1000 to a vote at the end of March where it secured a $526 million grant and loan guarantee for the project. Construction will begin later this year. The United States played a critical role in this process by both a $15 million financial contribution to CASA–1000 but also the political support and really working very closely with the World Bank, the Islamic Development Bank, and all the four CASA countries to get this project up and moving. And so we are very proud of our initiative and work in that area.

TUTAP is another project in the electricity line which is also having similar kind of results. Electricity for the first time is already flowing, for instance, from Uzbekistan to Afghanistan. In fact, most of the lights that come on in Kabul are thanks to the lights that are being supplied from the Uzbeks on those electricity lines.

Plans are underway now to connect these grids to bring electricity from Turkmenistan to Afghanistan, from Uzbekistan down to Afghanistan, and also from Tajikistan and then eventually connect at a substation in Afghanistan and transit over into Pakistan as well.

And so these are the types of new relationships. We know the traditional dynamics well here between Afghanistan and Pakistan, for instance. What we are also seeing now are these kind of conversations between their finance teams, their economics teams, their water and energy teams on price negotiations, on transmission, on electricity.

On TAPI, TAPI we still believe has the power to be transformative in changing the natural gas markets that connect this region. It is the reason we have been a strong supporter for years. I think there is a lot that you would need to happen in order to attract the kind of international oil companies and the international investment to secure the pipelines, and we are actively working with the Turkmen, for instance, for them to have the conversations that they would need to secure the financing, to secure the rights and the access to work with an international oil company to move a project like that forward.

But if these types of projects go forward, what is really telling for us and what really I think energizes us, frankly, is you have a way of really kind of changing the dynamic of Central and South Asia through the Af-Pak lens. And you are creating connections that give all of these economies in different ways many more options than they currently have, and it gives them more ways to strengthen their sovereignty and economic independence in the region.

Senator KAINE. Great. Thanks very much.

Additional questions for the first panel, Senator Risch?

Senator RISCH. Briefly. I wonder if one of you could tackle for me the relationship between Afghanistan and Iran and how much business they are doing back and forth.

Mr. BLANC. Senator, I do not have numbers with me about their business. I am not sure if one of my colleagues might. If not, we are happy to provide that for you.

Senator RISCH. I wonder if you could provide it, but also if you can give us a general sense at this point.

[The written reply by Mr. Blanc to the requested information follows:]

As a result of their geographic, linguistic and cultural connections, Afghanistan and Iran share significant trade ties, particularly in the Western region of Afghanistan and in Herat. Much of the trade practiced today between the two countries goes back generations. In recent years, Afghanistan-Iran trade has increased due to cost increases and customs delays for cargo transiting Pakistan in 2011, when the closure of the Ground Lines of Communication (GLOC) indirectly affected commercial traffic as well. Given these problems and the lack of other feasible transit options, many private Afghan traders opted to bypass the delays in Pakistan by moving goods through Iranian ports instead. Afghan imports transiting through and originating from Iran rose from $1.6 billion in 2011 to $2.7 billion in 2012 according to data from the United Nations. The number of Afghan exports to Iran remains very small, estimated by the U.N. at only $12 million in 2011 and decreasing to $8 million in 2012.

Understanding that Afghanistan continues to have limited transit options for accessing international markets, we have advised the Government of Afghanistan to exercise extreme caution in its trade with Iran to ensure that Afghanistan is not used by Iran to undermine the international community's effort to ensure Iran lives up to its international obligations. Where possible, we encourage Afghanistan to seek alternate trading routes. We have used diplomatic engagement and technical assistance to support implementation of the Afghanistan-Pakistan Transit Trade Agreement, which we hope over time will reduce barriers to Afghan access to Pakistani ports. We also continue to support Afghanistan's access via Central Asia, where U.S. investments in the Northern Distribution Network over the past decade have improved infrastructure and trade facilitation significantly.

Mr. BLANC. Maybe I will just answer a general question.

You know, I think that obviously there is trade between Afghanistan and its neighbors, including with Iran. And some of that is healthy and is necessary, and we encourage Iran to play a responsible role in Afghanistan.

One thing that we do consistently is to remind our Afghan partners about the nature of our sanctions against Iran so that when they make decisions about things, for example, work through the Chabahar Port, they understand the implications that that has because of the very strict laws we have in place.

Senator RISCH. Ms. Sumar.

Ms. SUMAR. I would reiterate that this is one of the toughest neighborhoods in the world, and so if you look in this context, you have Iran, Russia, China, and all the other tensions and relationships that you already have existing within the broader South Central Asia space. And so economic relationships that are already existing there, whether it is with the Iranians, the Chinese, the Russians, others in the region, those relationships continue to exist.

But I think in our diplomatic relationships that we have with these countries in terms of looking at ways to strengthen their economic independence, we continue to reiterate, you know, be careful in the decisions you are making so that you do not run afoul of United States sanctions on Iran, which are very important to us and one of our top priorities. Our policy on Iran is very well known in our relationships. It is a constant conversation that comes up in our relationships with these countries. And we have continued to engage India and others that engage on trade with Afghanistan via Iran, for instance, on Chabahar Port and others that their engagement needs to be in strict accordance with United States law and U.S. sanctions so that they do not run afoul of those issues.

So we can definitely, Senator Risch, come back to you with the actual statistics of trade between Iran and Afghanistan. But we definitely do it in our regional economic engagement work within a broader context of the kind of policy options that we would like to see.

Senator RISCH. Thank you.

Senator KAINE. I want to thank the first panel. Thank you very much for your testimony today. Ms. Sumar, you are going to be invited back now that you have survived the first witness experience, transitioning from committee staff to the witness table. Thank you all.

And I would like to invite the second panel to come up and we will jump right into this testimony. As the second panel is coming forward, I will just introduce them, and these are individuals who will be no stranger.

Gen. John Allen, U.S. Marine Corps, retired, is a distinguished fellow currently in the foreign policy program at Brookings, but as all are aware, prior to joining Brookings, General Allen commanded the NATO International Security Assistance Force and U.S. Forces in Afghanistan from July 2011 to February 2013. He has a long track record of service to our country before those assignments, but those are assignments particularly relevant to the hearing today.

In addition, we are fortunate to have with us Parnian Nazary. She lived in Afghanistan until 2004, a native, when she moved to the United States for her education. She is joining us today representing Women for Afghan Women. Ms. Nazary has always promoted Afghan women's rights through her involvement with various agencies working with Afghani women.

And I will say I have read a lot of written testimony in my 15 months in the Senate. Both of your sets of written testimony for very different reasons were particularly compelling, and I am glad to have you here today.

And I would ask General Allen to begin and then Ms. Nazary to follow.

STATEMENT OF GEN. JOHN ALLEN, U.S. MARINE CORPS, RETIRED, DISTINGUISHED FELLOW, BROOKINGS INSTITUTION, WASHINGTON, DC

Mr. ALLEN. Thank you, Chairman Kaine and Ranking Member Risch. It is an honor to appear before this subcommittee on this important subject of the future of Afghanistan in the post-2014 period.

Before I offer a brief statement, please let me thank the members for all that you continue to do for our magnificent troops in Afghanistan. As this year winds down to the close of the mission, I believe history will record well that the United States Congress on behalf of the United States people unfailingly supported our troops and our mission through very difficult years, and for that, Mr. Chairman, and to all the members of this committee and to the U.S. Congress, I will always be very grateful.

I would like to present my thoughts today on the future of Afghanistan in the form of a letter that I will be writing to the President of Afghanistan once he is inaugurated. And so it will take the form of correspondence, and it goes as follows.

"Dear Mr. President, please accept my sincere congratulations on your election as the President of Afghanistan. Your election represents one of the most historic moments in the modern history of your country: the peaceful transition from one elected government to another. Indeed, this act sets a precedent for a region where democracy and peaceful transitions are far more aspirational than realistic.

"I have been and remain, Your Excellency, one of the strongest advocates of Afghanistan. So it is in that spirit, sir, at your inauguration that I offer the following points for your consideration.

"First, sign the bilateral security agreement and, in so doing, embrace Afghanistan's desire for a long-term security relationship with the United States, NATO, and key partners. Seek to repair Afghanistan's relationship with the U.S. and the West. Here is your chance, Mr. President, to begin your Presidency in partnership and not in conflict with the nations who bled and spent their treasure on and for Afghanistan's people.

"Additionally, embrace your role as the Commander in Chief of the Afghan National Security Forces. They have demonstrated extraordinary feats of organization, development, and operational accomplishment. They are brave, principled, and ready to endure great hardship in following your orders and sacrificing for Afghanistan. And your forces need to see, and need to feel, your firsthand engagement and positive leadership.

"Second, protect the remarkable advances of civil society and, in particular, those of women. Much has been accomplished here, but often in spite of existing leadership, systems, and policies. The world is holding its collective breath in anticipation of what will become of the gains of women and minorities under your administration. Your public commitment to defending, furthering, and advancing women's and minorities' rights will be warmly welcomed by the international community, which is keen to help, but will also require a comprehensive strategy of Presidential decrees and legislative reforms to lock in these gains and to secure the future. As you well know, Mr. President, no state has ever successfully transitioned into a developing society without fully embracing the constructive role of women.

"Third, reach out to Pakistan. For myriad complex reasons, the relationship between your country and Pakistan and their respective peoples has deteriorated alarmingly over the course of this conflict. The absence of trust, compounded by uncertainty about the future, has left both nations to hedge their bets, to the good of no one and the detriment of all involved. Both nations share substantial common trade, economic, social and security interests. In that regard, I suggest you seek to reinvigorate the Afghan-Pakistan Transit Trade Agreement and support TAPI and pursue aggressively other cross-border and regional economic ties with Pakistan. As well, dealing with the alarming growth of extremists, terrorists, and insurgents on both sides of your common frontier should be a high priority and an important basis for constructive dialogue between your administration and that of Prime Minister Sharif in Islamabad. This dialogue can also serve as a platform for resolving the long-simmering issues over the Durand Line.

"Fourth, make Afghanistan business-friendly. As you build effective governance and reinforce the rule of law, initiate the necessary legal and regulatory reforms to leverage the natural entrepreneurial spirit of the Afghan people and to create a truly business-friendly environment to attract international businesses. The Tokyo Donors Conference in July of 2012 signaled a readiness of the international community to invest on the order of 16 billion U.S. dollars during the coming decade. This can be accelerated by the right reform package and your clear and public commitment to doing business within Afghanistan and externally within the region and with the international community.

"Last, but in the long term, most importantly, Mr. President, I urge you to undertake a sweeping, coordinated, and decisive counter-corruption campaign. Here time is not on your side. Acknowledging that the United States and the West bear some responsibility for the state of corruption in Afghanistan, the great challenge to Afghanistan's future is not the Taliban or Pakistani safe havens or even an incipiently hostile Pakistan. The existential threat to the long-term viability of modern Afghanistan is corruption. For too long, we focused our attention solely on the Taliban as the existential threat to Afghanistan. They are an annoyance compared to the scope and the magnitude of corruption with which you must contend. While the Afghan National Army will battle your nation's foes and in that context battle the Taliban, the battle for Afghanistan, the real fight, will be won by righteous law enforcement, a functioning judiciary, and an unambiguous commitment to the rule of law. Indeed, wresting back the institutions of governance from corruption must be one of your highest priorities. You know, Your Excellency, that corruption is the dry rot of democracy.

"In closing, Mr. President, I offer these points with the greatest respect. Your commitment to these five areas will be welcomed by the Afghan people who have endured so much, and your leadership in these areas will be hailed internationally. The future of Afghanistan is in your hands.''

I ask that this statement be read into the record, sir, and I am ready for your questions.

[The prepared statement of Mr. Allen follows:]

PREPARED STATEMENT OF GEN. JOHN ALLEN, RETD.

Chairman Kaine and Ranking Member Risch, it is an honor to appear before this subcommittee on this important subject of the future of Afghanistan in the post 2014 period. Before I offer a brief statement, please let me thank the members for all you continue to do for our magnificent troops in Afghanistan. As this year winds down to the close of this mission, I believe history will record that the United State Congress unfailingly supported our troops and their mission, and for that Mr. Chairman, I will always be grateful.

I'd like to present my thoughts today on the future of Afghanistan in the form of a letter I will be sending to the President-elect.

———

Dear Mr. President: Please accept my sincere congratulations on your election as President of Afghanistan. Your election represents one of the most historic moments in the modern history of your country: the peaceful transition from one elected government to another. Indeed, this act sets a precedent for a region where democracy and peaceful transitions are more often than not aspirational and not realistic.

I have been and remain, Your Excellency, one of the strongest advocates for Afghanistan. I have seen up close the nobility of your people, and I have a comprehensive appreciation for the potential of your country. You will have many competing priorities as you assume office, but please know the American people and the international community wish you every success, and wish for your people every opportunity to move beyond more than three decades of war to a future they and we have sacrificed so much to achieve.

It is in this spirit, President ---------, at your inauguration, I offer the following points for your consideration:

First, sign the Bilateral Security Agreement (BSA), and in doing so, embrace Afghanistan's desire for a long-term security relationship with the U.S., NATO, and other key partners. Seek to repair Afghanistan's relationship with the U.S. and the West. Here is your chance Mr. President to begin your Presidency in partnership—and not in conflict—with the nations who bled and spent their treasure on and for Afghanistan's people. Additionally, embrace your role as Commander in Chief of the Afghan National Security Forces (ANSF). They have demonstrated extraordinary feats of organization, development, and operational accomplishment. They are brave, principled, and ready to endure great hardship in following your orders and sacrificing for Afghanistan, and your forces need to see and feel firsthand your engaged, positive leadership.

Second, protect the remarkable advances of civil society, and in particular those of women. Much has been accomplished here, but often in spite of existing leadership, systems, and policies. The world is holding its collective breath in anticipation of what will become of the gains of women and minorities under your administration. Your public commitment to defending, furthering, and advancing women's and minorities' rights will be warmly welcomed by the international community, keen to be helpful, but will also require a comprehensive strategy of Presidential decrees and legislative reform to lock-in these gains and secure the future. As you well know, Mr. President, no state has ever successfully transitioned to a developing society without fully embracing the constructive role of women. Your many friends in the international community are ready to assist you in further empowering the role of women, and more broadly the role of civil society, in building legitimate and enduring institutions of governance.

Third, reach out to Pakistan. For a myriad of complex reasons, the relationship between your country and Pakistan, and their respective peoples, has deteriorated alarmingly over the course of this conflict. The absence of trust, compounded by uncertainty about the future, has left both nations to hedge their bets—to the good of no one and the detriment of all involved. Both nations share substantial common trade, economic, social and security interests. In that regard, I suggest you seek to invigorate the Afghanistan Pakistan Transit Trade Agreement and pursue aggressively other cross border and regional economic ties with Pakistan. As well, dealing with the alarming growth of extremists, terrorists, and insurgents on both sides of your common frontier should be a high priority and an important basis for constructive dialogue between your administration and that of PM Sharif in Islamabad. This dialogue could also serve as the platform for resolving long simmering issues over the Durand Line. Mr. President, the bottom line is that the Afghan and Pakistani people are in the same lifeboat, adrift in a sea of political turmoil, economic challenge, and extremist threat. Your collective approaches to these daunting problems will brighten the possibilities for both countries. Reaching out to Pakistan at the beginning of your administration is both courageous and timely, and will be strongly supported by the international community, including India.

Fourth, make Afghanistan business friendly. As you build effective governance, and reinforce the rule of law, initiate the necessary legal and regulatory reforms to leverage the natural entrepreneurial spirit of the Afghan people and to create a truly business friendly environment to attract international businesses. The Tokyo Donors Conference in July 2012 signaled a readiness of the international community to invest on the order of $16B USD during the coming decade. This can be accelerated with the right reform package and your clear and public commitment to doing business within Afghanistan, and externally within the region, and with the international community.

Last, but in the long run most importantly, Mr. President, I urge you to undertake a sweeping, coordinated, and decisive countercorruption campaign. Here time is not on your side. Acknowledging that the U.S. and West bear some of the responsibility for the state of corruption in Afghanistan, the great challenge to Afghanistan's future isn't the Taliban, or the Pakistani safe havens, or even an incipiently hostile Pakistan. The existential threat to the long-term viability of modern Afghanistan is corruption. Indeed, across your great country, the ideological insurgency, the criminal patronage networks, and the drug enterprise have formed an unholy alliance, which relies for its success on the criminal capture of your government functions at all levels. For too long, we've focused our attention on the Taliban as the existential threat to Afghanistan.

They are an annoyance compared to the scope and magnitude of corruption with which you must contend. While the Afghan National Army will battle your nation's foes, the battle for Afghanistan will be won by righteous law enforcement, a functioning judiciary, and an unambiguous commitment to the rule of law. Indeed, wresting back the institutions of governance from corruption must be one of your highest priorities, Your Excellency, for as you know, corruption is dry rot of democracy. Your fledgling institutions of government and governance and any real hope of economic development will be stillborn if the drug lords and CPN leadership remain in control.

In closing, Mr. President, I offer these points with the greatest respect. Your commitment to these five areas will be welcomed by the Afghan people who've endured so much, and your leadership in these areas will be hailed internationally. The future of Afghanistan is in your hands.

With abiding respect now and always, I remain,

JOHN R. ALLEN, *General, U.S. Marine Corps (Retired),*
Former Commander, NATO International Security
Assistance Force, and U.S. Forces Afghanistan.

Senator KAINE. Without objection. Thank you, General. Ms. Nazary.

STATEMENT OF PARNIAN NAZARY, ADVOCACY MANAGER, WOMEN FOR AFGHAN WOMEN, WASHINGTON, DC

Ms. NAZARY. Chairman Kaine, Ranking Member Risch, and other members of the committee, thank you for giving me the opportunity to speak today about the progress, challenges, and hopes of my Afghan sisters in this critical year of transition in Afghanistan.

Let me also thank you for your longtime support of the Afghan people and especially Afghan women.

The suffering of Afghan women, especially in the last three decades, is widely known and extensively documented by rights organizations. Some of us Afghan women became victims of war and insurgency, but let us remember and celebrate that many of us are survivors. Born and raised in war, my personal life is intertwined with the political struggles of my country, making my political and policy views inseparable from my story.

Many of you already know that under the Taliban regime, women were banned from education, employment, access to health care by virtue of being banned from visiting a male doctor, political participation, and many other basic rights. The Taliban had even banned women from appearing by the glass windows inside their own homes. In other words, Afghan women were not free inside their own homes, let alone in public.

I was barely a teenager when the Taliban took over Kabul in 1996. One of the first things they did was to close all schools for girls. During the Taliban regime, I could not enjoy simple things in life as a girl. I was denied basic things just because of my gender.

Yet, despite the Taliban's ban on girls' education, many brave women started secret schools in their homes. I enrolled in secret schools three times but each one was discovered and closed down by the Taliban. Every day I walked to the secret school with fear, as the Taliban had security checkpoints in almost every block. I hid my books in an unmarked bag and changed my route to school constantly.

In class were about 30 young girls. I was the youngest and did not have to wear a chaderi, a long cloth covering women from head to toe and imposed on all women over the age of 13 by the Taliban. However, once my classmates were inside the class, they would cast the chaderi aside.

We were enjoying our secret classes until one day a girl enrolled in my school burst into the room. The Taliban are coming, she screamed. Everyone rushed to grab their chaderi and wrapped up our books and whatever we could get our hands on. Some of us threw our books in the closet. Everyone was trembling as the Taliban blasted through the door and rushed in carrying whips and rifles. ''What are you doing here,'' one snarled. ''Learning to sew,'' one of our teachers said, her voice shaking. Pretending to sew was a backup plan in case the Taliban raided our secret school. As the Taliban saw an unstitched cloth in our hands, they hit the teacher with a whip.

Another Taliban gang man opened the closet and saw our books. He called shameless and dirty and tore our books into pieces.

The Taliban ordered all of us out of the building. Some passers-by pleaded with them to let us go. The Taliban finally let us go but took our teachers. I remember running home in tears, fear, and shock.

At age 13, I was stopped on the street and yelled that I should start wearing a chaderi outside now I was old enough. One day I was stepping out of home wearing a chaderi when I suddenly felt the burn of a lash on my back. I began to run. But the Talib religious police ran after me and hit me again and again. I still do not know what my crime was, but I only remember hearing ''palan tu kujas,'' the man beating me said in a heavy accent. Where is your skirt?

After these experiences, I refused to live under their rules, but at that age and in those circumstances, the best I could do was to wage a silent resistance. By myself, I started to study harder than ever because I knew I could only fight such an ideology through the power of education. My home became my school and I became my own teacher. The Taliban wanted to create a prison for me and with the help of my family, I created my own school.

My story is not unique. This was the situation for millions of Afghan women under Taliban rule.

In sum, the suffering was unspeakable. The pain was unbearable and the operation was unimaginable. And this is where Afghan women more forcefully started their fight for equal rights after the Taliban regime finally collapsed in 2001. And let me tell you, over the last 13 years the gains Afghan women have made are beyond anyone's wildest expectations. Afghan women have come a long way since the dark days of the Taliban regime, and all of this happened in just a little over a decade.

Yet, despite the immense progress, all the gains made so far remain fragile. With the U.S.-led coalition forces scheduled to leave by the end of this year, many Afghan women feel uncertain if their gains will be sustained without continued support from the international community. During my trip to Afghanistan last month, the one sentiment among all Afghan women was a shared fear of being abandoned by the international community while the Taliban insurgency continued to threaten women's hard-won gains.

The Taliban have not changed. They have become more complex. But they have not changed their views on education of women. Their targeted attacks on education, including schools, teachers, and students continue; prominent women's rights activists, including media, including singers, journalists, and musicians are well documented and continue.

Despite increasing attacks on Afghan women across the country, it does not stop them from fighting for their rights. I saw a picture of a woman voting in 2014 elections with her ring finger because her first finger was chopped off by the Taliban in 2009 elections. That is the fight of Afghan women and their bravery now. This shows the bravery of Afghan women who put themselves on the front lines and fight for equality, justice, freedom, and democracy.

While I was inspired by the progress made, I am most concerned with the future. Before discussing the specifics, I would like to make one point. As we all look toward the future, I would like to ask you to remember that a country cannot be built in 12 years or even 20. Afghanistan's development as a more stable, rights-respecting partner for the United States in an incredibly unstable region cannot be measured in years or election cycles. This is a process that will take decades and generations. My generation is the first of what will hopefully be many that has been educated and brought up in a largely democratic society. My generation has to be able to move forward toward the democratic foundations to firmly take root in the country. And for that to happen, the torch has to be passed to them, something which is taking place, but the sustained involvement and support of the international community is critical for it to be completed.

Looking forward, we understand U.S. civilian financial commitments will be significantly less than over the past 13 years. However, we need to know your support will not waver even if funding levels drop.

The bilateral security agreement, which has the support of almost all Afghans, will be signed by our new President I hope.

Some United States troops need to remain and funding must continue in order to allow my generation to complete the hard work of reclaiming Afghanistan from a generation of war and fundamentalism to a generation of hope and democracy.

Having considered this, I share with you a set of recommendations which I hope will help better shape support for the Afghan women beyond 2014. I have submitted four recommendations in my written testimony and am reading a snapshot of it here.

Firstly, for peace and justice, I have looked at extensively into peace talks with the Taliban and have reached a conclusion that reconciliation with the Taliban is fruitless. I am more than 100 percent convinced that any peace deal with the Taliban would most definitely compromise women's rights and their gains will be eroded away.

Two, ensure that women's rights remain central to the leadership between the United States and Afghanistan. In every conversation a United States official has with an Afghan official, he or she should mention the importance of women's rights.

Three, continue to invest in education and especially in higher education. Scholarships to study abroad for Afghan men and women and the American University of Afghanistan in Kabul are excellent examples of such an investment.

Four, continue to provide long-term support to Afghan civil society organizations, especially those involved in promoting women's rights.

Five, support the Afghan National Security Forces beyond 2014 in order for them to fight the Taliban insurgency and provide support for the Afghan men and women fighting for their rights.

Six, continued support for the Afghan media and freedom of speech.

Seven, support women's shelters, educational programs to highlight domestic abuse, and other social programs which tackle the multitude of issues facing Afghan women.

Thank you all for your support of Afghanistan. We would not be in the midst of a successful election or be here talking about progress made without you and the American people's immense sacrifice on our behalf. We are also grateful to our American sisters who have supported us and have stayed with us through the bad and the worst times. It is because of your support and sacrifices that we, the women of Afghanistan, have been empowered to fight for gains despite all odds against us. We are determined to move forward and strengthen the foundations for a better tomorrow and hope our friend and ally, the United States, will walk with us.

Thank you.

[The prepared statement of Ms. Nazary follows:]

PREPARED STATEMENT OF PARNIAN NAZARY

Chairman Kaine, Ranking Member Risch, and other members of the committee, thank you for giving me the opportunity to speak today about the progress, challenges, and hopes of my sisters in this critical year of transition in Afghanistan.

Let me also thank you for your long time support of the Afghan people and especially Afghan women. Without your support, the support of your colleagues and support from the people of the United States, Afghans would likely still be living under Taliban rule, deprived of everything, including basic human rights.

The suffering of Afghan women, especially in the last three decades, is widely known and extensively documented. Some Afghan women became victims of war and insurgency but we also must remember and celebrate that many of us are survivors. Born and raised in war, my earliest childhood memories from the 1990s include collecting golden and bronze bullet shells from my neighborhood in Kabul and building castles out of them. My personal life is intertwined with the political struggles of my country, making my political and policy views inseparable from my story.

I was barely a teenager when the Taliban took over Kabul in 1996. One of the first things they did was to close all schools for girls, leaving me and millions of other Afghan girls locked up in our own homes with no hope of receiving an education.

Even though things were not easy before the Taliban took over my city, I was still able to go to school and see my friends. But after the Taliban I was denied basic rights and opportunities because of my gender.

Yet despite the Taliban's ban on girls' education, many brave women started secret schools in their own homes. I was overjoyed when I found out about one such secret school in our neighborhood, Shar-e-Now. Even though my parents knew I could be harmed by the Taliban for attending school they agreed to enroll me.

I walked to school every day with fear as the Taliban had security checkpoints in almost every block. I hid my books in an unmarked bag and changed my route to school constantly.

Once inside the class, I was happy to see another 28 or so girls. I was not old enough to wear a chaderi, a long cloth covering women from head to toe, but the older girls did. They'd throw their chaderis to the side as soon as they'd stepped into the class.

We were enjoying our secret classes until one day a little girl studying with us burst into the room. "The Taliban are coming," she screamed.

Everyone rushed to grab their chaderi. Some of us wrapped up our books in whatever we could get our hands on. Some of us threw our books in the closet, hiding them under piles of clothes. Everyone was trembling as the Taliban blasted through the door and rushed in carrying whips, some of them with rifles hanging from their shoulders. "What are you doing here?" one of them asked. "Learning to sew," one of our teachers said, her voice shaking. The Taliban soldiers looked around and saw twenty or so girls with needles, threads, and cloth in their hands.

Pretending to sew was a backup plan in case the Taliban raided our secret school. One of the Taliban soldiers wanted to know why we wanted to learn to sew. Our teacher replied, "Because you do not let us go to a tailor shop and we want to learn to at least sew our own clothes." The Taliban gunman asked my classmates to show their work. All we had was unstitched cloth. He then hit our teacher with a whip.

Another Taliban gunman opened the closet and saw our books. He called us "shameless and dirty" and tore some of our books. I was in tears because my English vocabulary notebook was there too. I had spent so much time putting all of it together. My notebook also contained my drawings of girls studying by candle, something which perhaps made the Taliban gunman even more upset.

The Taliban ordered all of us out of the building. Some residents watching us pleaded with them to let us go, citing the Taliban's own edicts to be in presence of women without a moharam, an immediate blood relative. The Taliban finally let us go but took our teachers. I remember running home in tears, fear, and shock.

Months later, I learned about another secret school teaching English. I enrolled, but within a week or so I found a note behind the door which said the Taliban had closed down the school.

When I was old enough and had to wear the chaderi outside, I once stepped out in my neighbourhood wearing a chaderi, and suddenly felt the burn of a lash on my back. I began to run—the man hit me with second and a third lash. I still don't know why I had to be beaten on the street at age 13. I only remember hearing, "Palan tu kujas?"—"where is your skirt?"

After these experiences I refused to live under their rules, but at that age and in those circumstances, the best I could do was to wage a silent resistance. By myself, I started studying harder than ever because I knew I could only fight such an ideology through the power of education. My home became my school and I became my own teacher. Of course, I needed books, which were forbidden to girls. I asked my male relatives for books, including some in English. I also wanted recorded materials, CDs, DVDs, tapes. Since the Taliban did not allow these, I had to ask my families and friends traveling outside the country to bring me English movies or recorded books secretly. A few of them agreed to take the risk. My uncle brought me the movie "Titanic." It was the only English movie I had and so I watched it over and over, learning every single word. I even cut my hair to look like not Kate Winslette but Leonardo Dicaprio, the male star of the movie. At that age it seemed like a good idea, especially since I wanted to speak English just like he did.

After working on my English for 3 years, I started teaching it to seven young girls in our neighborhood. I practiced Urdu, Pashtu, and Dari by reading novels, poetry, and any book available. I memorized Suras of the Quran in Arabic and verses of Hafez poetry. I also became interested in arts and started painting, cooking, and knitting. The Taliban wanted to create a prison for me. Instead, I created my own school.

My story is not unique. Unspeakable suffering, unbearable pain, and unimaginable oppression were the norm for millions of Afghan women under the Taliban.

And this is where we started our fight for equal rights after the Taliban regime finally collapsed. Since then our accomplishments have been monumental, though we also know there is far to go.

In terms of education, there are millions of Afghan girls enrolled in primary, secondary, and high schools. Hundreds of thousands of girls have graduated from colleges and universities.

In terms of media, under the Taliban regime everything was forbidden except for one Taliban radio station, the content of which included announcing the new limits imposed on civilians by the Taliban's Department of Vice and Virtue, the religious police. For instance, they would announce the number of hands chopped, some of the hands were hanged in trees for public display, or forbidding white shoes since it would be disrespect to the Taliban's white holy flag. For entertainment, the radio program included reciting tarana, men singing Taliban poetry without music. The sound of the Taliban's chants was so mournful. Like other girls, I'd turn off the radio once informed of the new rules I had to obey in order to avoid being beaten on the street the next day. It's unfortunate that some of that dreadful Taliban poetry can now be found in a book published by the Taliban's former Pakistan Ambassador Mullah Abdul Salaam Zaef's book the ''Poetry of Taliban.''

But things have changed now. There are more than 70 TV network and hundreds of radio stations in Afghanistan. During my trip to Kabul in 2012, a young woman was singing and dancing on stage at an Afghan TV station for Eid celebrations. I thought this program, with the modernity and liveliness of it, was being produced outside of Afghanistan. But I was wrong; my family said this was being broadcast from a live concert in Kabul.

In terms of technology, the only tech equipment available to Afghan civilians were old fashioned analogue phones that were always monitored by the Taliban. We had no way of communicating with our fellow Afghans and no means of communicating to the outside world. The country had become a giant prison inclusive of public punishment and humiliation.

Today, almost 90 percent of Afghans have access to cellphone and over 6 million Afghans have access to the Internet, which was also banned under the Taliban regime. (CITE)

Access to health care has dramatically improved for Afghan women since 2001. Under the Taliban regime, child mortality rate in Afghanistan was the highest in the world. For example, one in every four children died before the age of 5. Today, it is 1 in 10, a dramatic reduction (NPR). Back in 2001, life expectancy was estimated by the United Nations to be around 45 for Afghans. Today, it has increased to 60 years, an astonishing improvement in just a decade. For comparison, it took four decades to achieve the same level of improvement in life expectancy in the United States from early 1900s to the onset of World War II (USAID).

In terms of employment, tens of thousands women work as government employees, in the private sector and as teachers, journalists, doctors, engineers, college professors, business owners, security officials and in many other public and private spheres.

Prior to 2001, political participation for women in Afghanistan was nonexistent. But today, women make up 28 percent of Afghanistan's Parliament, higher than the U.S. Congress where it's at 18 percent (World Bank). Afghan women have served as governors, district governors, and many other high profile positions since 2001.

Perhaps, the most striking indicator of increasing political participation for Afghan women came on April 5 of this year when around 7 million, or 60 percent of eligible voters, went to the polls to cast their ballots for a new elected leader. According to Afghan election officials, women made up 36 percent of voters. In the former Taliban stronghold of Kandahar province, women made up 10 percent of candidates running for provincial council seats. And during election campaigning, the presence of women in election rallies was something international media outlets could not ignore. The New York Times wrote: ''There is finally the sense here, after years of international aid and effort geared toward improving Afghan women's lives that women have become a significant part of Afghan political life, if not powerful.''

Aside from the elections, since 2001, Afghan women have taken the lead in organizing themselves as part of the growing Afghan civil society and fighting for their rights, at times successfully overturning laws which restricted women's rights. For example, Afghan women rights groups successfully fought the Afghan Government when it wanted to close shelters for battered women under pressure from Islamic clerics in 2011 (NPR). Another example was of Afghan women stopping the Afghan Government from including a new criminal penal code which barred family member's testimony in cases of domestic violence, effectively making it impossible to convict those accused of violence against women. My organization, Women for Afghan Women, took the lead on this and we lobbied the Afghan Government hard until President Karzai agreed not to sign the new bill into law, eventually sending it back to Parliament for further review.

In just over a decade, Afghan women have come a long way since the dark days of the Taliban regime. Yet despite the immense progress, the gains made so far remain extremely fragile. With U.S. led coalition forces scheduled to leave by the end of this year, the security situation in Afghanistan facing related uncertainty, and existing questions concerning future U.S. funding, many Afghan women question if their gains can be sustained.

I was in Afghanistan in February-March of this year and the one common sentiment among all Afghan women is their shared fear of being abandoned by the international community while the Taliban and insurgency continue to threaten our hard-won gains.

The Taliban continue to attack education. The U.N. reported more than 1,000 attacks on education in 2009–2012, including schools being set on fire, suicide bombings and remotely detonated bombs, killings of staff, threats to staff and abductions (Global Collation to Protect Education from Attack).

The Taliban have stepped up their attacks on prominent women in the Afghan Government and also in local communities. For example, Sitara Achakzai, a prominent Afghan women's rights activist was shot dead by the Taliban after leaving a provincial council meeting in Kandahar. Last year a Taliban attack targeted Islam Bibi, a top female police officer in Helmand province. Two other female police officers were killed within 6 months in 2013 in Laghman province in eastern Afghanistan. "Female police officers seem to be a favorite target of [Taliban] insurgents," (The Guardian).

Taliban's opposition to media and women's participation in public life is no less severe than it was a decade ago. For example, in 2012 the Taliban beheaded 17 people, including two women, for attending a mixed-gender party where there was music and dancing (ABC News).

Despite increasing targeted attacks on Afghan women and girls across the country, it has not stopped them from joining security forces or serving as public officials. While women are in the front lines of fighting for their rights, their success also depend on the continued support of the international community and the Afghan Government.

While I am inspired by the progress made, I am most concerned with the future. Before discussing specifics, I would like to make one point.

Since moving to the U.S. and having the opportunity to learn about the international community's interventions in countries such as Afghanistan, I am often struck by the short point of view policymakers are forced to adopt.

As we all look toward the future, I would like to ask you to remember that a country cannot be built in 13 years or even 20. Afghanistan's development as a more stable, rights respecting partner for the U.S. in an incredibly unstable region cannot be measured in years or election cycles. This is a process that will take decades and generations.

My generation is the first that has been educated and brought up in largely democratic society. Young Afghans, male and female, are better educated and more connected to the world than any generation before us. This was evident in the fact that 70 percent of the candidates for provincial council seats were youth (TOLO TV). Afghan media, which have witnessed an explosive growth over the last 13 years, are mostly run by youth. Mine is a generation full of hope but we also face incredible uncertainty as the international community prepares to withdraw from Afghanistan.

For my generation to be the force that allows democratic foundations to permanently take root in the country while eventually coming to power, progress and stability must be maintained as the torch is passed. This is now taking place but the sustained involvement and support of the international community is critical for the process to be completed.

Looking forward, we understand the U.S.'s civilian financial commitments will be significantly less than over the past 13 years. However, we need to know your support will not waver, even if funding levels drop. The Bilateral Security Agreement, which has the support of almost all Afghans will be signed by our new President, some U.S. troops need to remain and funding must continue in order to allow my generation to complete the hard work of reclaiming Afghanistan from a generation of war and fundamentalism to a generation of hope and democracy.

Having considered this, I share with you a set of recommendations which I hope will help better shape support for the Afghan women beyond 2014.

(1). The Taliban, their supporters, and the like-minded groups across the region continue to pose a threat to women's social, legal, economic, political and basic rights. Based on the experiences of Afghan women activists, the Taliban have refused to show any changes toward the treatment of women since their fall from power in 2001. In case of any peace talks with the Taliban, all parties involved must be extremely cautious of the fact that a peace deal with the Taliban would compromise women's rights and erode their gains.

(2). It is vital that women's rights remain central to the relationship between the U.S. and Afghanistan: To preserve the gains of Afghan women, the U.S. must continue pushing Afghan politicians and diplomats to do the right thing. As a funder, ally and partner, the U.S.'s role in Afghanistan hopefully will not soon disappear; meaning every conversation a U.S. official has with an Afghan official should mention the importance of women's rights.

(3). While millions of Afghan girls have been enrolled in primary schools since 2001 (USAID), it's important to continue investing in education and to further invest in higher education for women through scholarships, technical programs and other educational opportunities beyond 2014. Afghanistan's next generations will depend on continuation of such support.

(4). Continued support for Afghan civil society organizations, especially those involved in promoting women's rights: Through strategic investments and mentorship many women leaders have been brought up in Afghanistan. Continuing to support such agents of change and progress will encourage the continued transformation of Afghan society.

(5). Supporting Afghan National Security Forces beyond 2014: I believe one cannot support women's rights, human rights, or development in Afghanistan without also supporting a strong ANSF because security is the foundation from which all Afghan progress can grow and be sustained. We at Women for Afghan Women believe it's vital some U.S. led international troops stay in Afghanistan, supporting and training our military while also symbolically assuring the Afghan people they won't again be abandoned by the international community. This also means continuing to fund the ANSF. I know this is not cheap ($4 Billion annually +/-), but it is necessary.

(6). Continued support for the Afghan media and freedom of speech in Afghanistan. The explosive growth of Afghan media and the rapid rise of freedom of press have been two key and major gains of the last 13 years. Afghan media have also played a critical role in enabling democratic principles to take root in Afghanistan.

(7). Supporting women's shelters, educational programs to highlight domestic abuse, and other social programs which tackle the multitude of issues facing Afghan women.

Thank you all for your support of Afghanistan. We would not be in the midst of a successful election or be here talking about progress made without you and the American people's immense sacrifice on our behalf. We are also grateful to our American sisters who have supported us and stayed with us through the bad and worst times. It's because of your support and sacrifices that we, the women of Afghanistan, have been empowered to fight for gains despite all odds against us. We are determined to move forward and strengthen the foundations for a better tomorrow and hope our friend and ally the United States will walk with us.

Senator KAINE. Thank you very much, Ms. Nazary.

Six-minute rounds and we will go until we need to vote or until witnesses have other commitments. I will begin.

General Allen, we hear different assessments of the current status and strength of the Afghan National Security Forces, depending on whether we are in intel meetings, foreign relations meetings, armed services meetings, depending on whether we are talking to NGOs that are active in Afghanistan. Your letter that you intend to send to the President delved into that a bit, but I would like your candid assessment of both strengths and continuing challenges with the ANSF in your view.

Mr. ALLEN. Thank you for that question, Senator.

I think the case is clear that in almost any developing security force, the more technical dimensions of that force are always going to be a challenge.

As well, there will be the challenge associated with the development of leadership. The substantial challenges which I faced as the commander and I believe still will be a challenge for some sometime in the future will be ensuring that the Afghan leadership are well prepared and developed, they are continually improved in their capabilities by the long-term presence of our forces on the ground in an advisory capacity, that the institutions of the schools and the training centers are well equipped and poised to continue the upward development of the Afghan leadership because without credible Afghan leadership at all levels, from the general officers through the mid-grade down to the youngest of the troop commanders, the Afghan National Security Forces will hit a glass ceiling very early. So the leadership development is a really important dimension of what we are doing.

And more work simply needs to be done. We typically found that the officer corps had deep roots in one of three eras: the Soviet era, the mujahideen era, and then the modern era, the era where we would see young Afghan officers, men and women who look like our young officers, who are professionally oriented in the same manner. And they are the hope of the future. But as you know, it takes time obviously for them to ascend through the ranks.

In the meantime, doing as much as we can in an advisory capacity, we have to work with the Soviet era officers, those officers who have been developed over a period of time who have fewer skills and less education. The mujahideen jihadi leaders are an example of that. So the officers are an area which deserves our continued attention and for as long as possible our long-term touch of that aspect of the Afghan society.

And then the technical dimensions. It is one thing to conduct infantry operations. It is another thing to support infantry operations. So everything from the logistics support, the combat service support, the air movement locally by helicopter movement or by fixed wing transport, all of these require technical abilities. And as those capabilities are more profoundly placed into the hands of the Afghans over time, that kind of training regimen is going to be important to ensure that they have the ability to exercise those capabilities.

When I was the commander, at the beginning of my tour in July 2009—excuse me—July 2011, we saw very few large-scale operations being accomplished in Afghanistan because of the inability of the staffs to plan them and execute them and the inability of the organization to support them. As I was departing—and I know as of last year—we were routinely seeing corps level operations occurring across Afghanistan where numbers of regiments or brigades would be in the field being supported routinely by the logistics of that organization.

Now, that is a huge improvement from where we were, but that improvement has to continue. There has to be a long-term touch of those forces to continue that upward spiral. An advisory presence— I may well get the question in any case—I think is essential to the long-term capacity of the Afghan National Security Forces to create the security platform on which we hope to see credible governance and real economic opportunity occur. That will occur with the right kind of advisory presence.

And it is not just about the numbers. It is about the presence. I have been involved in training of foreign forces for many years and I have been an advisor. Just our presence in their ranks provided the connectivity of the moral support of the American people and, more broadly, the international community. It means that the lives of these Afghan troops matter because we are with them and we are in their ranks. So advisory presence is not just about imbuing them with the technical skills or the tactical skills. It is about being simply with them.

And so much work remains to be done. We have got to keep our hands on the officer development program because the Afghan National Security Forces will never better than their officers. But there is much technical work remaining to be done. As we continue to flow technically oriented equipment into the hands of the Afghans, we have got work to be done there.

Senator KAINE. Thank you.

One question for Ms. Nazary, then to Senator McCain.

Ms. Nazary, your recent visit to Afghanistan coincided with the period of the first round of the Presidential elections. Tell me what the Afghan population desire is with respect to women's empowerment issues you describe. Was it a key feature of the campaigns and is the popular support strong for continuing on the path of progress and battling against backsliding if there are those who want to reverse course?

Ms. NAZARY. In all of the public debates, all the candidates spoke about their support for Afghan women's rights, and even up to the very last debate, Dr. Ghani emphasized the support for Afghan women's rights. So that has been seen very widely, and I think during the elections, the people were very enthusiastic in Afghanistan. In their rallies, there were more people coming and everyone watched the debates. It was the first Presidential debates we had so openly. So it was a great joy to be there and see that.

Senator KAINE. Thank you for that.

Senator McCain.

Senator McCAIN. Thank you, Mr. Chairman.

I thank the witnesses.

General Allen, one of the great pleasures of my life, as well as honor, is to be associated with people like you who are such outstanding leaders, and your work in Afghanistan, in my view, and before that in Iraq, has been incredibly honorable. And I thank you for your continued service to the country, and I thank you, Ms. Nazary, also.

Obviously, the reason why I am very interested in hearing your views is we seem to be seeing, in my view, a replay of what happened in Iraq when we ended up without troops there.

There was an April 21 piece that says United States force in Afghanistan may be cut to less than 10,000 troops. I remember there were some leaders that said that the minimum should be 20,000, and then it seemed to be the coalescing around our military and Ambassador and others, 10,000 plus 3,000 or 4,000 additional

NATO troops. Is that pretty much the way you have seen this evolve?

Mr. ALLEN. Yes, sir. Sir, as you recall, my recommendation on the U.S. side was 13,600 U.S. and about 6,000 non-U.S. NATO and partner nations.

Senator MCCAIN. Right. And now we are in a situation where it seems to be—as General Dempsey once testified before the Senate Armed Services Committee about the numbers in Iraq, it cascaded down. It seems to be cascading down.

Here again, according to this article, the decision to consider a small force, possibly less than 5,000 United States troops reflects a belief among White House officials that Afghan security forces have evolved into a robust enough force to contain a still potent Taliban-led insurgency. Do you share that view?

Mr. ALLEN. I do not, Senator. Look, the Taliban are going to be a potent and resilient insurgency for a long time. The question is whether they are an existential insurgency.

From my perspective, an Afghan National Security Force that is well advised and well supported, which gives us the time to lock in these leadership traits and technical capabilities and battlefield skills, that will ultimately put the end to the insurgency in Afghanistan. They have not had the time. The Afghan National Security Forces have not had the time to embrace a culture of leadership, to embrace the technical dimension of modern warfare, or to, in fact, embrace the ability to fight in large formations on the battlefield. That will come over time. Our presence, a credible presence, with those forces is what will lock in that success and lock in that security platform.

Senator MCCAIN. And that credible force is what you just stated.

Mr. ALLEN. That was my recommendation.

Senator MCCAIN. Then it goes on to say during a March visit to Washington, General Dunford told lawmakers that without foreign soldiers supporting them, Afghan forces would begin to deteriorate, "fairly quickly in 2015." It goes on. "The Afghan Air Force, still several years away from being self-sufficient, will require even more assistance," he said. Do you share that quote from General Dunford? That view.

Mr. ALLEN. Well, again, Senator, I do. I believe from my own personal experience, both in Afghanistan and in Iraq, in Bosnia, in other places, the accepted, enthusiastic presence of foreign forces in the formations of an emerging youthful force—it is an essential presence frankly.

And at the end of the Soviet era, we learned two lessons. One was that the Soviets left advisors with a pervasive touch across the Afghan forces that had been provided by them. Now, you might have problems with the Soviets or have problems with the Afghan forces, but in the end, they were a pretty effective force. And the Soviet decision was to leave substantial numbers of advisors and a substantial resource trail of money to support that force.

When the Soviet Union began to come apart and the advisors first were withdrawn and then when the Soviet Union collapsed and the money was withdrawn, we saw ultimately the very rapid deterioration of the post-Soviet Afghan force. It began to collapse, fragment along ethnic and tribal lines, and we saw from that the emergence of the civil war and all of the horror that Ms. Nazary has talked about.

Our recommendations were predicated upon having a sufficient advisory presence and a long-term funding stream to give us the time to prepare the Afghans and to lock in those skills so that they on their own, as they ought to on their own, will be the authors of the stability of Afghanistan over the long term. That is why this campaign has always envisioned—it has always envisioned—a residual force that would carry on the work at an advisory level that we paid such a high price to pay for in the conventional phase.

So I do agree with General Dunford.

Senator MCCAIN. And you would think that we might have learned a lesson from Iraq, but perhaps not.

I guess, finally, it is pretty obvious it is going to be Ashraf Ghani or Abdullah Abdullah as the next President of Afghanistan. You have had a lot of conversations and engagement with both of those individuals. Do you have confidence in both of them?

Mr. ALLEN. I have confidence in both of them, sir. Dr. Abdullah Abdullah—and I want to be careful with my public comments not to appear to influence the runoff if it comes. I will limit my comments that I have known Dr. Abdullah Abdullah for some period of time. I think he is a very responsible leader with great governmental experience. I worked very closely with Dr. Ashraf Ghani because he was the coordinator for the process of transition. He also is a former minister and has had extensive experience.

The value of both of those candidates, frankly, is that they are extraordinary well educated. They are well connected into the Afghan society across tribal and ethnic lines. They are well accepted and well known by the international community, and I believe, very importantly, they hold very similar views on the long-term presence of the West and the value of that presence both for civil society, the rights of women, and the long-term security stability. I believe they are also, very importantly, committed to what I think is the existential threat in Afghanistan and that is rooting out corruption.

Senator MCCAIN. I thank you, General Allen. And I know you have also been involved in other issues, including the Israeli-Palestinian issue, and I thank you for your continued service to the country.

Thank you, Mr. Chairman.

Senator KAINE. Thank you, Senator McCain.

Ms. Nazary, a question about youth activism. General Allen talked about the need to train the military leadership with young leadership coming up through the ranks. Talk a little bit about the engagement of the Afghan youth in the election process that you just observed. With that average age being age 18, a lot of our hopes about the future of Afghanistan rests with the leadership of that generation, those who are 18 to your age. And talk about their degree of political participation in this recent first round of the Presidential elections.

Ms. NAZARY. I think the Afghan population is—about 70 percent of the population is under the age of 25. So that actually gives me great hope for the future of Afghanistan. I know of Afghans my generation who have come to study abroad or in Afghanistan and have been extremely active. For example, Afghanistan 1400. It is the year 1393 in Afghanistan. So 1400 is looking ahead. And it is a youth coalition built in Afghanistan by the youth, and they are very politically active and make informed choices of who to vote for. This is something that gives me real hope.

Senator KAINE. Thank you for that.

General Allen, I want to ask a question about Pakistan. You heard the first panel when I asked the question about the economic opportunities with Pakistan, and Ms. Sumar offered some thoughts about how a number of projects could potentially sort of change what has been the complicated dynamic you described. Do you have the same hope about those? Do you have concerns? What is your current thought about that piece of advice that you will give to the next President on the Afghan-Pakistan economic relationship?

Mr. ALLEN. Well, I think that the new President and his administration in Kabul really gives us an opportunity to reach out to the Sharif administration in Islamabad to create a new era of cooperation. That cooperation, as I said in my opening statement, can come in many ways, but one of the most important opportunities for cooperation is economic cooperation. I think we all know from our study of history and our study of insurgencies that you fight an insurgency to a certain point in a military context, but you lock in the gains of governance and economic opportunity by stimulating economic growth, economic relationships, and regional trade.

My sense is that Prime Minister Sharif grasps that. He said important things about improving the relationship with India, and part of that improvement is not just a political relationship but it is an economic relationship as well. So by tying in the Central Asian states to the emerging economy of Afghanistan—and we do not really know yet what that economy looks like. It has been distorted by 30-plus years of crisis and conflict. But by tying in the Central Asian states and their wealth to the emerging Afghan economy, ultimately to a willing and receptive Pakistani system of government which is at a policy level willing to have the relationship with Afghanistan, and then have that transit across Pakistan to India creates an opportunity for economic development in that part of the world that we just cannot begin to imagine.

So my hope is that the new President in Kabul will reach out to his counterpart in Islamabad and deal with the issues of security and the people-to-people dynamics, but the opportunity for economic advantage for both countries, if they can see that same common interest, I think is really important.

Senator KAINE. I want to ask you a question about your last piece of advice dealing with what you view as the existential threat, corruption. You indicated that the West and the United States may have made the problem worse to some degree, and yet most of the challenge is a domestic challenge for the President and the new leadership team to deal with. Let me ask you about the piece that is on the U.S.'s side of the equation. While we can and will continue to encourage anticorruption efforts, are there lessons learned from the last decade that the United States should put into practice as we contemplate the kinds of aid whether it is international development or trade or other economic assistance that we provide to Afghanistan going forward? What improvements should we be looking to make on our own side of the equation?

Mr. ALLEN. Chairman, this deserves a lot of analysis because the knockout blow in insurgency is not delivered by the military. The knockout blow is delivered by the development of credible governance and economic opportunity. What we have discovered in Afghanistan—and I believe other Afghans would agree with me—when all of the institutions, recognizable institutions, of governance and the rule of law and the judiciary were crushed, after year after year either though the Communist coup or the Soviet era or the civil war or the Taliban period, the one thing that typically was functioning was the tribal system. And the patronage networks, which are inherent in a tribal system anywhere in the world, ultimately took on a far greater role in Afghan life than the systems of government and recognizable institutions.

It is going to be very difficult to root them out of the government and root them out of the institutions of government that they have sought to continue to influence because in many respects the struggle in Afghanistan, beyond the struggle in the battlefield against the Taliban—the struggle will be building credible governance at the expense of the criminality and the criminal patronage networks and the corruption. The criminal patronage networks see that a well-functioning government, a well-functioning judiciary, one that is based truly and credibly on the rule of law is in direct competition. So the struggle is not necessarily apparent to those who are observing what is happening in Afghanistan.

This swath of Afghan youth are fed up with corruption. They are fed up with having to pay a bribe to have their daughters or their spouses seen by physicians. They are fed up with having to bribe their way into schools. We have a swath of the youth of Afghanistan that is poised and ready ultimately to throw off the burden that corruption has placed on that society. And unless the administration of the newly elected President is willing to comprehensively go after the criminal patronage networks and the drug enterprise, often protected as we have seen in other insurgencies by the ideological Taliban right now, the ideological insurgency, we are going to have a problem over the long-term viability of Afghanistan.

So lessons learned. Ensure that as we dedicate development money and expend development money—ensure that the vetting process is proper and that the vetting process goes as deeply into the Afghan fabric or the host nation's fabric of society as we can to ensure that none of that money is siphoned off by subcontractors, sub-sub-subcontractors and ultimately find their way into the hands of the Taliban.

If I were to design a campaign like this all over again and we had the time to get it right, I would have looked very, very hard at the kinds of authorities necessary and the organizational approaches that give us the ability to achieve synergy between our intelligence organizations, law enforcement, and threat finance organizations to create synergy that permitted us to get at what is emerging really as an unholy alliance in many respects, which is the criminal patronage network operating in conjunction with the money-generating effects of the drug enterprise, supported by, protected by the ideological insurgency, the Taliban.

We have seen this elsewhere and we are going to see it again elsewhere. Going into a campaign well organized with the right kinds of authorities so that we can conduct law enforcement, counternarcotics, counterdrug work as we are doing counterinsurgency gives us the ability to tap into the strengths of all of those organizations. But in some respects, we firewalled those capabilities, and there was no cross-pollination that could have permitted us to build the synergy necessary to take that triangle apart and to attack the component legs of that triangle.

So lesson learned for me if I were ever to advise someone again about a long-term counterinsurgency that we might be involved in, it would be, first and foremost, recognize that the threat will be corruption inherently. It always will be, that there will be a drug component most likely, and that the two of those legs will be in some form of a symbiotic relation with the insurgency itself. Let us go in organized with the right kinds of legal authorities for the military, the police, the drug enforcement entities, the intelligence, and the threat finance. Let us go in with the right kind of organization, which I sought to do in my final months there as the commander, to let us get at probably the greatest threat to our success in that next insurgency, which is the insipient criminality that will exist once we have washed away the insurgency itself.

Senator KAINE. Ms. Nazary, I would like your opinion on the very same question. As you travel and interact with Afghan women and Afghan society, talk to me about your thoughts about this future anticorruption challenge in Afghanistan.

Ms. NAZARY. I think corruption is a challenge, and with the candidates, they all have again spoken that they will step up their efforts to work against corruption and I hope they will succeed in that.

Senator KAINE. And do you have that same sense that young people coming up have come up in a way where they are ready to cast off the notion of having to pay a bribe to see a doctor, having to pay a bribe to get into school?

Ms. NAZARY. That is very true, getting into school, getting jobs and opportunities. There is corruption and we see that, and people are fed up by that. Youth are fed up by that. And the civilians would very much want that to go away.

Senator KAINE. There is much that we can do and should do. Your testimony about us continuing our focus and engagement is very important, but the thing that is ultimately going to be the best guardian of success is that demand of the public that things be different, the demand of the Afghan public that things be different.

Very, very good testimony. Again, both of your written testimony was quite provocative and informative, and your personal testimony today was as well. I appreciate all being here.

The record of this hearing will stay open until close of business 1 week from today. So if committee members have questions that they wish to submit in writing, they will be submitted to you, and I hope you will respond promptly if they do.

But again, thank you for appearing on this important topic.

With that, the hearing is adjourned.

45

[Whereupon, at 11:56 a.m., the hearing was adjourned.]

ADDITIONAL MATERIAL SUBMITTED FOR THE RECORD

RESPONSE OF JARRETT BLANC TO QUESTIONS SUBMITTED BY
SENATOR ROBERT MENENDEZ

Question. Section 602(b) of the Afghan Allies Protection Act of 2009 authorized the issuance of Special Immigrant Visas (SIVs) to Afghan nationals who were employed by or on behalf of the U.S. Government in Afghanistan and who meet certain requirements. What percentage of SIV recipients are translators or security personnel? What percentage of SIV recipients are locally employed political officers or program support staff?

Answer. Since the start of FY 2014, the Department of State has issued over 1,900 Special Immigrant Visas (SIVs) to Afghan principal applicants, for a total of over 4,000 issued SIVs this year including eligible family members. This is more than all the previous years combined and more than double the total number of Afghan principal applicants issued visas in FY 2013. Of those total numbers, Afghans employed on behalf of the U.S. military, including translators and security personnel, continue to comprise the majority of SIV applicants. According to National Visa Center data on occupations as reported by SIV applicants, over 6,500 of those who have applied for the SIV program and received Chief of Mission (COM) approval to date reportedly worked as translators and another 200 as security personnel. Locally employed (LE) staff employed by the Department of State in Afghanistan have received 196 SIVs since 2012, with the vast majority (172) issued since October 2013. To date, 714 LE staff have submitted SIV application letters. These applications represent all aspects of the work done by LE staff, both those assisting with political issues and those in more traditional support staff roles.

RESPONSES OF FATEMA SUMAR TO QUESTIONS
SUBMITTED BY SENATOR ROBERT MENENDEZ

Question. How does the New Silk Road initiative work to develop the capacity of civil society watchdog organizations in Central Asia as countries in the region are encouraged to deepen economic ties across borders?

Answer. USAID's Development through Regional Cooperation (DRC) program supports the New Silk Road initiative's work with civil society. The DRC is a regional initiative covering all five Central Asia countries, with expanding participation of Afghanistan and Pakistan civil society organizations (CSO). The program is strengthening their watchdog and advocacy capacity in key thematic areas such as environmental issues, women entrepreneurship and children's rights. The program seeks to identify, network, and strengthen these CSOs from across the region in order to generate grassroots domestic constituencies for reform and while linking them to advance integration between Central Asian countries, as well as between Central and South Asia.

Question. How has the NSR sought to develop links among women business leaders in Afghanistan with their counterparts in South and Central Asia?

Answer. To increase women's economic participation, the U.S. Department of State and USAID support a number of programs which link women business leaders with each other to expand market opportunities and exchange business best practices.

For instance, the Department of State supports two regional initiatives: the Central Asia and Afghanistan Women's Economic Symposium (WES) and the South Asia Women's Entrepreneurship Symposium (SAWES). Now in its third year, the WES initiative has trained thousands of women and helped hundreds to obtain new or larger loans, establish or expand businesses, and gain employment in Central Asia. As part of the WES initiative, we are expanding women's markets and strengthening local production capacity through international textile trade hubs in Kazakhstan and the Fergana Valley situated across Uzbekistan, Kyrgyzstan, and Tajikistan. The initiative also helped launch the Central Asia Afghanistan Business Women's Network, which is the first regional women's business association to promote business, border, and trade reforms helpful for businesswomen across Central Asia and Afghanistan and has been operating for over 2 years.

The SAWES initiative is continuing efforts to empower women entrepreneurs through regional cooperation in South Asia and beyond. As a direct result of knowledge gained at the 2012 Symposium, the Afghan delegation established an advocacy group called ''Leading Lady Entrepreneurs of Afghanistan for Development'' (LEAD) in July 2013 to ensure businesswomen's voices are heard by policymakers. Through a series of cross-border training, advocacy, and networking activities, the initiative is helping to increase access to finance, markets, and business capacity for Afghan women entrepreneurs and develop connections with businesswomen across the region. For example, in April 2014, Afghan businesswomen, including LEAD members, participated in a regional study tour to Bangladesh where they gained experience in leadership skills, sustainable business models, advocacy tools, and access to financial support.

With U.S. support, Afghan women participate with Central Asians in business training at the Aga Khan Central Asia University and are able to attend the American University of Central Asia in Bishkek. Since 2010, USAID's Central Asian Trade Forums have brought together business and government representatives from the CAR countries and their counterparts from Afghanistan and Pakistan, including women entrepreneurs and organizations such as the Women's Development Agency in Tajikistan. In February 2014, the Afghan-Kazakh-Uzbek business-to-business conference in Mazar-e-Sharif attracted businesswomen and businesswomen's associations and led to commercial agreements in cosmetics and textiles. Moreover, since 2012 USAID's Women's Leadership in Small and Medium Enterprises (WLSME) program in Kyrgyzstan has worked with nearly 600 women entrepreneurs to build better linkages with suppliers, buyers and regional markets. In July 2013, USAID announced the Promoting Gender Equity in National Priority Programs (Promote), a 5-year program (2014–2019) to enable Afghan women to increase their participation in the formal economy by securing higher education opportunities and employment with advancement potential as well as establishing and expanding viable small- to medium- to large-sized women-owned businesses. Planned activities will coordinate closely with other USAID and donor projects, such as the regional economic growth project Afghanistan Trade and Revenue Project (ATAR), designed to address Afghan women's economic empowerment in-country and regionally.

Question. How much assistance funding has the State Department and USAID dedicated toward the goals of the New Silk Road Initiative since its announcement?

Answer. We are thankful for Congress' support for regional programming between Afghanistan and its neighbors in South and Central Asia. This type of programming, which we call the ''New Silk Road Initiative,'' is critical to supporting the development of a prosperous and stable Afghanistan embedded in a prosperous and peaceful region. Since 2011, the New Silk Road initiative has coordinated and intensified efforts by the United States, donors and regional stakeholders to advance regional economic connectivity. For the past 3 years, we have aggressively employed diplomatic and development means to facilitate Afghanistan's economic transition through regional connectivity between South and Central Asia and the broader region.

The State Department and USAID have committed more than $24.3 million in regional Central Asian Economic Support Funds (ESF) to support targeted interventions with funds from fiscal year 2012 through fiscal year 2014. These funds have been and will be used to increase trade and investment; improve transit; advance cooperation on energy trade; promote effective management of natural resources across the region; and develop sustainable people-to-people constituencies for regional engagement on private sector and trade development.

In addition to these regional resources, bilateral resources from Afghanistan, Pakistan and the Central Asian Republics have supported regional connectivity priorities. For instance, in the area of trade, USAID has leveraged resources from the Regional Economic Cooperation (REC) project in Central Asia, the Afghanistan Trade and Revenue (ATAR) project and the Pakistan Trade Project (PTP) to work toward the common goal of facilitating trade across a traditionally unconnected region. ATAR alone has committed nearly $8 million toward cross-border programming between Afghanistan and Central Asia.

Infrastructure projects funded with ESF resources in Pakistan have built multiple roads linking Afghanistan to Pakistan and the broader region, including all four major trade and transit routes including Peshawar-Torkham, Quetta-Chaman, Bannu-Gulam-Khan, and Angoor Adda. The Pakistan TRADE project has also worked to boost regional trade and has reduced the time in Karachi port for Afghan goods in half, from 43 to 23 days.

Recognizing the importance of cross-border trade and transit between Afghanistan and Central Asia, we have undertaken a comprehensive effort to ensure that regional and related bilateral activities are properly coordinated and function to promote regional trade and investment and security. We have made investments in core infrastructural assets such as roads, aviation and telecom, laying the foundations to help promote interconnectivity with the people, businesses and countries of Central Asia. Substantial investments have also been made in power generation and distribution that will further enable economic development as well as promote domestic, regional and foreign investment and enhance regional stability.

Notably, we have also successfully leveraged other resources in support of the New Silk Road initiative; between fiscal years 2010 and 2014, estimated investments by other donors, total more than $2 billion, including the Asia Development Bank and the World Bank, in support of energy transmission lines, hydropower plants, and energy-sector reforms. Specifically, with Central Asia regional funds, USAID's Regional Energy Security Efficiency and Trade Project has spent over $4 million to fund the CASA–1000 Inter-Governmental Council Secretariat which coordinates planning on a $1 billion, 1,300 megawatt electricity transmission line which will connect Central Asian countries with Afghanistan and Pakistan.

Question. Does the Department of Defense have a role in the New Silk Road initiative? If so, how has the State Department worked with DOD to support the goals of the initiative?

Answer. The New Silk Road initiative relies on interagency cooperation to realize the shared objective of a stable, secure, and prosperous Afghanistan as part of a stable, secure, and prosperous South and Central Asia. The Department of Defense is one of many interagency partners that have aided the New Silk Road's focus on regional economic cooperation. Support has included extensive programs building the border capacity between Afghanistan and Pakistan and Central Asia as well as assistance on energy and trade facilitation. Their support includes both infrastructure, such as installation of rail scanners on the Uzbek-Afghan border at Termez, as well as technical assistance to facilitate secure, regional trade flows.

Looking beyond the economic and security development work, our Department of Defense colleagues have an instrumental role in developing and maintaining the Northern Distribution Network (NDN) and its supply chains throughout Central Asia that supported operations in Afghanistan. These endeavors leverage mentoring and other assistance USAID, the European Bank for Reconstruction and Development (EBRD) and other partners provided to businesses. The relationships and expertise gained through Department of Defense efforts in Central Asia are critical aspects of continued New Silk Road engagement in the region. We continue to work with our Department of Defense partners on identifying ways to incorporate NDN lessons learned within New Silk Road efforts. In late April, State and Defense personnel met at the Defense Logistics Agency in Ft. Belvoir to review further ways to transition NDN for commercial use throughout the region. The New Silk Road will remain a platform for the Department of Defense and other interagency partners to pursue our shared objectives regarding Afghanistan's future in the South and Central Asia region.

———

RESPONSES OF KATHLEEN CAMPBELL TO QUESTIONS
SUBMITTED BY SENATOR ROBERT MENENDEZ

Question. Does USAID provide support to Afghan civil society organizations that conduct oversight on Afghan Government ministries which also receive U.S. support? If so, how many organizations receive funding and at what levels? Please describe the programming conducted by these organizations.

Answer. USAID funds activities by a wide range of Afghan civil society organizations whose work relates to overseeing Afghan Government performance. These activities are generally organized around types of services or issues that often are the responsibility of more than one Afghan ministry, such as monitoring provincial level corruption and promoting women's rights.

USAID funding for civil society-specific programming in FY13 was $60.2 million, including $14.4 million in women's-specific programming. The Agency's principal civil society support program has facilitated capacity building for 374 Afghan NGOs across the country as part of a civil society support network. Other programs regularly involve engagement and capacity building with civil society groups, including USAID's parliamentary support program, media program, rule of law program, and work on stabilization and democracy.

There are some cases where funding civil society organizations is designed to increase the accountability and effectiveness of government programs that also receive USAID funding. For example:
- *Elections:* USAID has invested $25 million during this election cycle on programs to support civil society capacity-building around advocacy for electoral

reform. Through these efforts, civil society organizations (CSOs) are helping to hold the Independent Election Commission (IEC) and the Independent Electoral Complaints Commission (IECC) accountable for decisions relating to election planning, security, and complaints. The United States also supports the IEC and ECC with a $55 million contribution to the $129 million UNDP-administered ELECT program that pools funding from multiple donors.

- *Rule of Law:* USAID has supported the Afghanistan Independent Bar Association (AIBA) through a multiyear, $1.2 million grant, which provides legal aid and legal awareness services to indigent Afghans who need representation in court. At the same time, a component of USAID's Formal Justice Rule of Law program provides support to the Supreme Court to train judges and improve court administration so that access to justice can be improved.

More generally, USAID's two largest and most comprehensive civil society programs are the Initiative to Support Afghan Civil Society (IPACS II), which concluded at the end of 2013, and the follow-on Afghan Civic Engagement Program (ACEP), which started in 2013 and runs through 2018. IPACS II strengthened a national Afghan civil society network of 374 local NGOs, many of them women-led or women-focused CSOs, to improve their capacity in areas such as leadership, governance, strategic planning, gender awareness and mainstreaming, sustainability, and monitoring and evaluation. Through these civil society strengthening efforts, CSOs were able to, for example:

- Engage in advocacy and monitoring of the Afghan national budget process and launch an annual national policy reform conference;
- Advocate with Members of Parliament for the adoption of 29 of 33 amendments to the Social Organization Law, amendments that President Karzai signed into law in September 2013;
- Advocate for changes to nine articles of the government's proposed law on Non-Governmental Organizations, which are being considered by Afghanistan's Ministry of Justice;
- Advocate for and become signatories to a Memorandum of Understanding between Parliament and civil society organizations; and
- Bring together civil society organizations, local government authorities and individual citizens to identify local challenges and develop local solutions through 1,286 Community Dialogue Sessions in 30 provinces, involving more than 25,738 people. These dialogues feed into a national level effort to prioritize civil society's policy reform efforts and advocate these priorities to the Afghan Government.

ACEP, USAID's follow-on civil society and media program, will continue this important support to anticorruption and government oversight activities that utilize civil society organizations, the traditional media and social media to educate citizens against corruption. ACEP will promote greater CSO engagement with government and policymakers, as well as oversight, through trainings in legislative processes, policy research, constituency-building, networking, transparency/anticorruption, lobbying and monitoring of service-delivery, to its 14 key partner organizations and their 140 CSO partners in the provinces.

In the first year of the program, ACEP plans to award four Government Monitoring and Policy Advocacy Campaign Grants with estimated grant ceiling of $43,000–$45,000 per grant, to the following organizations:

- Afghanistan Development and Welfare Services Organization: The Build Demand for Accountability project will work with selected government institutions to develop a business process map (charter) for their administrative services used by citizens. The project is designed to address the lack of awareness amongst citizens on the established timeframes for government services as well as the document flow process and the roles of various government offices.
- Afghan Coordination Against Corruption: AFCAC proposes to work with the Ministry of Education (MoE) on this project that is designed to stimulate the creation of an anticorruption culture at the ministry level. The project will advocate for the implementation of an anticorruption action plan.
- Integrity Watch Afghanistan: The project will carry out qualitative research in four provinces (Kabul, Nangarhar, Balkh, and Herat) on the intended and potential role of CSOs in the provincial budgeting process. It will raise CSOs' awareness on budget issues through technical trainings and will build networks of CSOs at the subnational and national levels to work on provincial budgeting issues.
- Initiatives for Development (IDO): IDO proposes to implement the project in collaboration with Empowerment Center for Women (ECW) with the goal of launching a civil society advocacy initiative aimed at improving Government

service delivery and promoting accountability through monitoring National Budget spending and the performance of the five line ministries.

Question. On May 5 the Washington Post published a story which described a lack of USAID oversight on a major grantee, International Relief and Development (IRD). Please provide information about IRD's hiring and executive compensation practices and its use of nondisclosure agreements for USAID funded programs in Afghanistan.

Answer. USAID conducts annual ethics training for all of its employees on post-government employment rules and requirements, with a particular focus on new employees and those planning to leave Federal Government employment. Post-government employment rules generally do not prohibit former employees from working for any particular company. However, officials who leave the Agency are prohibited from representing a new employer back to the Federal Government on particular matters, for example on a contract on which the former employee worked.

As a nonprofit entity, International Relief and Development (IRD) primarily receives grants and cooperative agreements as opposed to contracts. Compensation costs, such as executive compensation, are generally reimbursable under United States Government (USG) awards if they are reasonable, allowable, and allocable per governing regulations. For nonprofit entities such as IRD, annual A–133 audits are required in accordance with the Office of Management and Budget requirements. The A–133 independent auditors are responsible for determining the propriety of costs claimed under USG awards, including executive compensation and bonuses. IRD's rate calculation and supporting data included in the A–133 audit do itemize certain costs, but do not delineate executive compensation separately from other labor costs. Aggregate bonus costs are broken out as a line item, and are not delineated by employee. A–133 audit results are shared for review with USAID, including the Office of Inspector General. Recent A–133 audits of IRD did not question executive compensation or bonus costs or identify any other items of questioned costs.

With regard to USAID's grants and cooperative agreements, separate efforts have been undertaken to reiterate the whistleblower protections provided to employees of assistance recipients and subrecipients. On May 9, 2014, USAID sent letters to all assistance recipients regarding their statutory obligations to notify and observe the legal protections afforded their employees. Concurrently, a Procurement Executive Bulletin was issued to all USAID Contracting and Agreement Officers to ensure that the applicable provisions related to whistleblower protections were included in all new and existing awards. USAID contractors and implementing partners have an obligation to report allegations of waste, fraud, or abuse related to USAID projects. No contractor or partner should use nondisclosure agreements to limit the federally protected rights of its employees to report waste, fraud or abuse.

Question. All of these factors inhibit transparency of U.S. foreign assistance and make the external coordination of aid dollars even more difficult.

USAID's Foreign Assistance Dashboard features transaction-level data for Afghanistan, but does not include performance data.

♦   Why isn't data published on the Dashboard linked to performance data?

The State Department does not publish its foreign assistance data on the Dashboard, creating an incomplete picture of U.S. assistance efforts in Afghanistan.

♦   Why doesn't the State Department publish its foreign assistance data on the Dashboard?

U.S. agencies involved in foreign assistance do not use the International Aid Transparency Initiative (IATI) XML format to publish their data; instead their data is "crosswalked" from the Dashboard into the IATI standard, often compromising the integrity of the data.

♦   Why don't USAID and the State Department use the IATI XML format at the outset to publish their data?

Answer. The Foreign Assistance Dashboard (FAD) is a Department of State-managed Web site that presents budget, obligation, and disbursement data for all U.S. Government agencies that have foreign assistance funding. The purpose of the FAD is to make U.S. Government foreign assistance data available to the public in open, machine readable formats and to enable anyone to track foreign assistance investments in a standard and easy-to-understand visual format. USAID submits data to the FAD in accordance with the mandates in OMB Bulletin 12–01, which provides guidance on the regular submission of timely, detailed, high-quality comparable data on foreign assistance disbursements. The FAD is not a performance Web site, and OMB Bulletin 12–01 does not require agencies to publish performance data on the FAD. USAID, however, does publish performance information in several other places, and links disbursement data from the FAD and Afghanistan's annual performance data on its Dollars to Results (http://results.usaid.gov/) Web site. USAID will incorporate FY 2013 data on the Dollars to Results Web site before the end of the third quarter. Other publication of performance data include our Annual Performance Plan and Report as part of the Congressional Budget Justification, on Performance.gov, on USAID's Open Data Listing (http://www.usaid.gov/data), and in evaluations which are available online through the Development Experience Clearinghouse (http://dec.usaid.gov).

In the U.S. IATI Implementation Plan, the administration publically committed to have all U.S. Government foreign assistance data reported on the FAD by the end of 2015. USAID has provided the FAD with budget data since December 2010. In 2012, USAID began providing aggregate obligation and disbursement data, and in July 2013, USAID became the first U.S. Government agency to fully comply with OMB Bulletin 12–01 and release detailed transaction-level data to the FAD. Our Department of State colleagues can provide details on their schedule for providing the Department's information as well as the status of other agencies reporting to the Dashboard. OMB Bulletin 12–01 does not require agencies to report data in the XML format directly to the FAD at this time. USAID data are submitted to the Department of State in an Excel file, which is then converted to XML using crosswalk mapping that USAID developed, cleared, and believes in no way compromises the integrity of the data. The Department of State then registers the data with IATI, allowing USAID's transaction-level information to be available in XML on the FAD "Data" page.

Question. Family Planning.—Globally, we are seeing a skyrocketing demand for family planning services. In the most vulnerable populations, we see both a high birth rate due to cultural influences, and a high number of maternal deaths linked to backroom abortions.

♦   What is USAID doing to promote family planning services in the most vulner- able populations and how do you plan to address the social and religious barriers?

Answer. USAID's family planning and reproductive health program contributes to lower maternal and child mortality by enabling women to choose the number, timing, and spacing of their children and by reducing unintended pregnancy, thereby reducing abortion. We utilize mobile outreach and frontline community health workers to provide voluntary family planning information, services and referrals to women and men in hard-to-reach and rural areas. We ensure that HIV-positive women and men have access to quality counseling and family planning services through the integration of voluntary family planning and HIV services. In addition, our partnership with other donors has allowed us to negotiate lower unit prices for the most in-demand contraceptives, reducing financial barriers and increasing access to a wide range of contraceptives for women with an unmet need for family planning. We support the provision of a wide variety of family planning methods, including nonhormonal methods, in all USAID-assisted countries.

USAID supports innovative interventions to help individuals and communities address social and religious barriers, which hinder access to family planning, including harmful gender norms. USAID's programs work with local support systems, health providers, and traditional leaders to educate families and communities about the critical importance of family planning for the health of both the mother and the child. In Afghanistan, USAID trains and empowers community and religious leaders and local organizations to deliver health messages and build community awareness about the need for women, and particularly young women, to have access to family planning services. In Yemen, USAID collaborated with local religious leaders and the Yemeni Ministry of Public Health and Population to conduct a "Safe Age at Marriage" program, and provided integrated family planning and maternal and child health services to almost 300,000 clients.

USAID recognizes that youth must be reached to transform harmful gender norms, and that youth themselves have a particular unmet need for family planning information and services. All USAID-supported family planning and reproductive health programs address youth health in some capacity. In Afghanistan, USAID's work strengthens the ability of family planning service providers to tailor services to vulnerable populations, including young couples, and increases the availability of youth-friendly family planning services. In Nepal, USAID supports a national campaign that targets hard-to-reach key audience—including youth, young couples, migrants, and the socially excluded—with messages to promote informed choice and improve method and service use among clients. The campaign also includes a range of activities promoting the acceptance of family planning among community and religious leaders.

_____

RESPONSES OF FATEMA SUMAR TO QUESTIONS
SUBMITTED BY SENATOR TOM UDALL

Question. The New Silk Road initiative has undergone an important transformation from a vision to an action plan economically linking the countries of South and Central Asia. While the primary focus area, energy, does have the ability to accelerate development in the region, it will be difficult to fully take advantage of Central Asia's hydropower potential and build new capacity without addressing the tensions around water-sharing that have existed for decades. The U.S.-Mexico International Boundary Water Commission has been essential in resolving issues around boundary demarcation, national ownership of waters, water quality, and flood control in the border region.

♦ What is the scope for similar institutions in the region and how is the Depart- ment supporting them?

♦ How is transboundary water management integrated into the energy planning pillar of the New Silk Road?

Answer. Although water is essential to Central Asia's economic growth, regional management of transboundary water resources is weak and a source of political tension. Improved management could diffuse tensions over regional water resources and unlock cooperation on energy issues. With our international partners, we are building capacity to manage transboundary water issues broadly throughout the region with technical training, diplomatic engagement, and institutional support. This includes providing funding to the U.N. Regional Centre for Preventive Diplomacy in Central Asia (UNRCCA), which has shown modest progress on developing a negotiated legal framework for managing transboundary water. We hope to contribute to the Central Asia Energy-Water Development program, a World Bank multidonor trust fund that is improving the regional capacity for managing water. Our efforts complement the efforts of the International Fund for Saving the Aral Sea (IFAS), the regional organization tasked with managing transboundary water issues. However, IFAS' nebulous organizational structure has impacted its efficacy, as have regional political rivalries that are often unrelated to water and energy. The increasing engagement of all five Central Asian nations and Afghanistan in these programs indicates we are incrementally improving cooperation on transboundary water management, and moving closer to the sustainable management of existing surpluses of summer hydropower to be exported over the Central Asia-South Asia (CASA–1000) power transmission project—a signature project of the New Silk Road. Our continued support of these programs will be the key to success.

Question. As the region and donors embrace economic cooperation as a necessity, and the Department continues to identify specific activities to advance the New Silk Road, the efficient use and decisionmaking around foreign assistance allocated to the region is more important than ever. This brings the Department's complex foreign assistance architecture into question. As it currently stands how are the separate SRAP, ACE, SCA and USAID foreign assistance units coordinating project-level decisions when each have separate funding streams with subregional or single country mandates?

♦ a. Are there efforts to streamline these functions to better support the New Silk Road initiative and the region as a whole?

♦ b. How would you recommend that the Department work to better focus plan- ning and expenditures for programs supporting the initiative as a whole?

♦ c. How are DOD-funded activities incorporated into your planning?

Answer. The Department of State, the U.S. Agency for International Development, the Department of Defense, and other interagency partners coordinate to pursue a shared objective: a stable, secure, and prosperous Afghanistan economically integrated with its South and Central Asian neighbors. The New Silk Road (NSR) initiative is the policy and operational framework for interagency cooperation to achieve the strategic objective of regional connectivity. NSR diplomatic and programmatic assistance activities focus on four core pillars: trade, energy, customs/borders, and people-to-people connectivity. Funding requests and programming are designed in the context of broader U.S. foreign policy interests, and aligned through bilateral and regional assistance strategies.

Given the cultural, political, and strategic complexity of the South & Central Asia region, the discrete competencies and mandates of a variety of agencies and bureaus are required to advance U.S. national security and economic interests. We have ensured that these activities are well coordinated and aligned through a variety of mechanisms, such as biweekly interagency working group meetings with Washington and field participants, regular phone calls to missions and communications with designated points of contact, including the Department of State, USAID's Asia Bureau and OAPA and DoD/CENTCOM, as well as monitoring activities of other donors and working with international financial institutions to allow us to track funding streams, report progress, share information, and avoid duplication of effort.

The Special Representative for Afghanistan and Pakistan (SRAP) coordinates U.S. Government-wide policy for national security, diplomacy, and assistance for those two countries in close cooperation with USAID's Office of Afghanistan & Pakistan Affairs (USAID/OAPA). The Department's Bureau of South and Central Asia Affairs works in close partnership with SRAP and the Asia Bureau in USAID to coordinate diplomatic and development work for South Asia and Central Asia. The Office of the Coordinator of Assistance to Europe, Eurasia, and Central Asia (EUR/ACE) and its Central Asia assistance mandate is integral to coordinating NSR-related regional and bilateral assistance activities linking Central Asia, Afghanistan and its neighbors. Within USAID, a formal intra-agency framework known as the "Almaty Consensus" guides the design and implementation of development programs in regional trade, energy and commerce which dovetail with the NSR initiative's four priority pillars.

The diplomatic and development vectors of the NSR initiative are augmented by close cooperation with the Department of Defense, which supports training and programs that improve border capacity and security between Afghanistan, Pakistan, and Central Asia. DOD is also instrumental in working to assist local businesses that formed the supply chains throughout Central Asia critical to logistical operations in Afghanistan through the Northern Distribution Network (NDN) to make the transition to compete in a nonmilitary, post-2014 marketplace.